Negotiating SPACES

The Lives of Undocumented Youth

Rodolfo Jacobo

Kendall Hunt
publishing company

Cover image © Shutterstock, Inc.

Kendall Hunt
publishing company

www.kendallhunt.com
Send all inquiries to:
4050 Westmark Drive
Dubuque, IA 52004-1840

Para/To
Isabella
Diego
Cristian
Karina
Mama y Papa
y todos los que buscan un rincon en este mundo
and all those who are searching for a space in this world.

Table of Contents

List of Figures and Tables

Foreword

Throughout the United States, undocumented students live in constant fear of their legal status being disclosed and, despite their educational success and professional objectives, face uncertainty and an unknown future.

This study has put forward the question: What are the effects of the symbiotic relationship of a historical anti-Mexican sentiment and a failed U.S. immigration policy on the negotiation of spaces by college-age Mexican-origin undocumented students?

The study research question asked: What are the existing social-psychological forces that shape the daily-lived experiences and negotiated spaces of unauthorized youth, in particular, those pursuing access to higher levels of education in the United States?

The conceptual framework of the study used two dimensions. The first consisted of explicit and implicit modes of behavior. The second dimension focused on how students navigate between regulated and unregulated spaces in their communities.

From a pool of thirty-six, eight unauthorized college age students participated in the study. The criteria for selection included being a Latino/a bilingual, bicultural, and bi-literate college-age student attending a two-year or four-year college/university in Southern California and living in the United States as undocumented residents for at least twelve years.

Qualitative case study methodology served to document the lived experiences of unauthorized youth using interviews, autobiographies, and face-to-face meetings. Data on each of the eight participants were analyzed to identify themes. The interactive process with participants consisted of data collection, data display, reflection on the data, data coding, data reduction, generation of themes, and thematic interpretation.

The findings derived from triangulated qualitative approaches informed the study on how unauthorized youth consistently negotiate their lived spaces. One moment they may be gifted college students in an unregulated legal space (college campus), and the very next they are committing a federal crime by living in the United States unauthorized (outside of the college campus).

Eight themes described the explicit and implicit tensions of lived space: identity, membership, micro-aggressions, trauma, resiliency-adaptability, pragmatism, agency, family, and structural violence. Furthermore, four additional concepts described their regulated and unregulated legal space in the form of social-psychological trauma, namely living in ambivalence, encapsulation, dissonance, and rejection.

Given that both the U.S. and the Mexican governments have done little to stop the flow of unauthorized immigration, accentuating the economic benefits of both nations, the study provides recommendations for further research. Specifically the recommendations relate to the human condition of unauthorized college-attending youth and discourse over the criminalization and virtual internment of undocumented youth in the United States.

Acknowledgments

I would like to first acknowledge my mother, Elena Jacobo, who regrettably did to get to witness this achievement. My mother had almost no formal education, but she was always clear about the importance of it in our lives. For thirty years she worked in the agricultural fields of California to give her children "una vida mejor." She gave us that and much more. Espero que en el cielo sonrias mama al ver cosechada tu siembra. My father, Rodolfo Jacobo Sr., has been my most unrelenting supporter, always cheering me on.

To my wife, Karina, I am grateful to share every part of my life with you. My children Isabella Diego, and Cristian your smiles make this life so much more beautiful. My brothers, Joel and Arturo, and their wonderful families have been nurturing and supportive, each in their own way.

My friends, Allison and Mario, this is as much yours as it is mine. Mario, only you and I could make the doctoral program seem like the first grade all over again. My mentors, Tom Davies, Isidro Ortiz, Richard Griswold Del Castillo, Rafaela Santa Cruz, Alberto Ochoa, Lourdes Arguelles, and Mike Ornelas, thank you all for your guidance. I want to thank Prisca and Elizabeth for all the coffee. To the students in this study, I am humbled by your fortitude.

Chapter 1

Statement of the Problem

The criminalization and virtual internment of undocumented youth in the United States is the result of historical prejudice and a failed immigration policy that condemns youth into a lifetime of uncertainty. The impact of past injustices and a failed immigration policy is painfully visible in the schools of our nation where undocumented students live in constant fear of their status being disclosed and where, despite their educational success, their dreams and professional objectives often seem futureless.

In mid-2005 it was estimated that there were some two million undocumented students in schools in the United States, with an estimated 65,000 graduating from high school every year (Horwedel, 2006). Existing law established by the Supreme Court case *Plyler vs. Doe* in 1982 gives undocumented children the right to a K–12 education under the Fourteenth Amendment of the U.S. Constitution. The court, however, never extended that right to higher levels of education (Horwedel, 2006).

While the Plyer federal court's decision is supportive of the right of undocumented children to attend school, it also handicapped the students by capping their educational access. The right of undocumented youth to attend college has produced a bitter debate throughout the United States on the issue of access to higher education and undocumented students. It is estimated that there are some 50,000 undocumented students in United States colleges (Horwedel, 2006). If we consider that 57 percent of the general undocumented populations are Mexican nationals, we may deduce that Mexican undocumented youth are highly represented in this group (Diaz-Strong and Meiners, 2007).

When the issue of immigration rights is discussed, often the main argument of access to education rests on the cost of benefits to the undocumented population. This discourse over the rights of immigrants, especially from Mexico, is not new. The educational rights of Mexican-origin children in general and of the undocumented in particular have

1

historically been at the center of the immigration debate. A clear pattern of discrimination against the Mexican-origin population and the marginalization of their children are historically evident (Jacobo, 2006; Soja, 2007; Velez-Ibanez, 1996).

To those who are concerned with the development of the human condition, the discourse over access to higher education by undocumented students generates a number of questions. Among the questions are: What is the symbiotic relationship of an historical anti-Mexican sentiment, a failed U.S. immigration policy, and the negotiation of spaces by Mexican-origin undocumented students? What are the historical and existing sociopolitical forces that shape the daily negotiation of lived spaces for these youth? How do unauthorized youth negotiate daily-lived situations? What are the psychological effects on undocumented youth?

This study examined the lived spaces of selected unauthorized college-aged youth. These youth, on a daily basis, confront their sense of identity, belonging, psychological emotions, and living spaces.

Conceptual Framework

This study was guided by a conceptual framework based on legal, sociological, and psychological concepts that seek to document explicit and implicit lived spaces (Shiner, 2008) of unauthorized Latino youth living in the United States. Two dimensions drive the conceptual framework of the study: (1) a legal dimension of immigration social policy, and (2) a socio-psychological lived space. Figure 1.1 illustrates the conceptual framework using the two dimensions of law and social psychological lived space.

The legal dimension is expressed from a legal continuum—at one end are unauthorized and unregulated social policy where the individual is able to negotiate his/her lived space by being very familiar of his/her surroundings. At the other end of the spectrum is unauthorized and regulated social policy where the individual in public spaces runs the risk of being apprehended for not having legal documentation.

The socio-psychological lived space dimension is expressed as explicit lived space and implicit lived space. The explicit lived space is what the individual is willing to share or is known to him/her and others. The implicit lived space is what the individual is not willing to share with others that s/he interacts with.

In the case of undocumented youth/students living in the U.S., the framework offers four quadrants of analysis. In Quadrant I (unauthorized

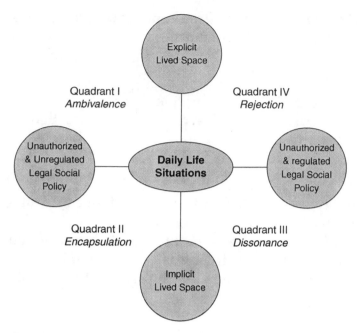

Figure 1.1 Conceptual Framework

and unregulated legal social policy and explicit lived space), the undocumented youth experiences ambivalence.

Under Quadrant II (unauthorized and unregulated legal social policy and implicit socio-psychological lived space) the undocumented youth experiences encapsulation.

Under Quadrant III (unauthorized and regulated legal social policy and implicit lived space) the undocumented youth experiences dissonance.

Under Quadrant IV (unauthorized and regulated legal social policy and explicit lived space) the undocumented youth experiences rejection.

Using the described conceptual framework, the study seeks to examine the existing socio-psychological forces that shape the daily-lived experiences and negotiated spaces of unauthorized youth, in particular, those pursuing access to higher levels of education in the United States. The conceptual framework serves as a tool for understanding the lived spaces and trauma experienced by unauthorized youth in the United States.

The framework allows us to analyze how unauthorized students navigate from an explicit to an implicit lived space and from a regulated to an unregulated legal space. The framework suggests a way to measure variance in social integration. Moreover, it reveals the types of trauma experienced by unauthorized youth such as stress and depression, emotional distress, and having no sense of legal assurance.

Research Question of Study

The study is guided by the following question:

What are the existing socio-psychological forces that shape the daily lived experiences and negotiated spaces of unauthorized youth pursuing access to higher education in the United States?

To answer the main research question, three sub-questions were explored:

- What are the types of daily-lived situations that confront undocumented youth sense of identity and belonging?
- What types of psychological trauma impacts how undocumented youth negotiate their daily-lived situations?
- How do Latino undocumented youth respond to the daily psychological trauma that they experience?

Significance of the Study

This study provides insights into the unauthorized student population pursuing a college degree in the United States, their lives, aspirations, and resiliency. Scholars, educators, immigration reform advocates, and those against immigration reform can reflect on the conditions and personal trauma experienced by college-aged unauthorized students. The findings may lead to more informed positions and reforms in education, social, and immigration policy.

This study offers a unique gaze into the lives of young people who live in the shadows of American society. All their lives, they have had to navigate social circles aware at all times of their legal status in the United States. In most cases, they were young children when they were brought unauthorized to the United States. Their parents, some legal, some not, were hopeful that immigration reform would one day provide their family with legal status in the United States. Unbeknown to them, they were placing their children in a perilous situation.

Despite the many obstacles faced by these youth, one finds them resilient and determined to succeed. They understand the value of higher education and are hopeful that the laws of this country will allow them to live out of the shadows. Unauthorized youth will benefit from this work, as it further advances the dialogue with the larger American society on the issue of access to higher levels of education and immigration reform.

Assumptions of the Study

The study assumed that the selected participants were representative of the unauthorized college-age student population and their lived experiences.

The study assumed that border communities of Southern California are one of the most policed geographical areas in the nation. Some examples include military bases, border check points, Immigration and Customs Enforcement (ICE) raids, as well as the existence of a conservative political arena.

The study assumed that federal policies, such as Operation Gatekeeper, and California state policies, such as AB 540, as well as Proposition 187, heighten the tension over immigration reform. In 1994 Proposition 187 denied undocumented persons any public services. While the proposition was found unconstitutional, it highlighted the debate over illegal immigration. AB540, a conditional legislation in California, allows selected undocumented to be treated as resident students.

The study assumed that the push and pull of economic forces are at work and that people seek to move from one country to another without legal documentation in search for a new life and to improve their economic condition.

Limitations of the Study

This study was limited in its sample size. This study was designed as narrative research involving eight college-age unauthorized Latina/o students of Mexican ancestry, who have been in the United States for most of their lives.

The participants were selected from the region of Southern California, where a significant number of unauthorized persons of Mexican ancestry reside.

The political climate in the country and the anti-immigrant sentiment can reduce the willingness of participants to fully describe their lived experience.

The legal status of participants and the creation of trust and willingness to be open about their lived situations can limit full disclosure of their personal feelings.

Operational Definitions

AB540 is a California law passed in 2001 that allows unauthorized California high school students who meet its criteria to pay in-state tuition for education in the state colleges and universities. These students must meet the following criteria:
a. Attend a high school in California for three or more years.
b. Graduated from a California high school or attained the equivalent.

c. "Alien" student must file an affidavit with the college or university stating that s/he has filed an application to legalize or as soon as s/he is eligible.

Coping skills are the various ways an individual positively or negatively confronts complex situations produced by his/her illegal status.

Daily-lived situations are everyday activities that an individual may undertake, such as going to school, driving, shopping, attending social events or recreational activities, or interacting with others in selected parts of the community.

Negotiated lived behaviors responses are presented in four dimensions and are defined as:

- **Ambivalence** is the living in a state of negotiating emotions in both positive and negative balance or actions in contradiction with each other, a feeling of uncertainty and indecisiveness. It is related to an individual who is familiar with his/her surroundings and has a high degree of awareness of civic behavior, while understanding his/her legal status and while interacting in low-risk social activities.

- **Rejection** is living in a state of conflict with his/her surroundings and feeling excluded from civic participation at the local, regional, and national level and understanding his/her legal status. It is related to an individual who is exposed to surroundings where s/he is visible and has no control of possible interactions or events.

- **Encapsulation** is living in a state of constant fear known only to him/her or intimate others and understanding his/her legal status. It is related to an individual who is constantly aware that s/he must always be on the lookout and must negotiate the lived spaces that offer him/her a sense of control.

- **Dissonance** is living in a state out of harmony within the community and within the self while understanding his/her legal status. It is the inability to feel part of a community and a feeling of helplessness and distance. It is related to an individual who is aware of where s/he is but has no control of possible interactions or events.

Regulated legal social policy is the active enforcement of individual's legal status whereby the individual's illegal status prohibits or controls mobility.

Unregulated legal social policy is an inactive enforcement of an individual's illegal status. Tensions arise when an individual's rights are protected under the "due process" and "equal protection" clauses of the Fourteenth Amendment of the U.S. Constitution.

Trauma is a psychological perspective that includes the feeling of fear, stress, depression, exclusion, and apprehension as a result of having unauthorized legal status.

Unauthorized students are students who are illegally in the United States and who are pursuing higher education based on state polices, such as California's AB 540 legislation.

Explicit lived spaces are open and visible interactive spaces and deliberate behaviors that are exhibited or known publicly (Robert, 1957).

Implicit lived spaces are hidden and not visible interactive spaces that are unrecognized to others or the public (Robert, 1957).

The study is divided into seven chapters. Chapter one provides the overview of the study. Chapter two describes salient research literature on immigration with a focus on the Mexican transnational community and dependency on Mexican labor over the years, as well on the phenomena of unauthorized undocumented students. Chapter three describes the methodology used in this study. Chapter four establishes the context of being undocumented via a personal reflection. Chapter five is a biographical piece of the eight selected college-aged students of Mexican ancestry with regards to living undocumented in the United States. Chapter six discusses the findings of the study and implications, and chapter seven provides recommendations for further research.

Chapter 2

Review of the Literature

Thematically, the symbiotic relationship of a historical anti-Mexican sentiment, a failed U.S. immigration policy, and the negotiation of lived spaces by Mexican-origin undocumented students is the subject of this literature review. The objective is to uncover the historical and existing sociopolitical forces that shape the daily negotiation of lived spaces for college-age undocumented youth.

Organizationally, the first section uses historical sources, the blatant, painful, and often-violent discrimination suffered by the Mexican-origin population by guided discriminatory policy and practices of the dominant Euro-American society (Acuña, 2007). The second part addresses the failed American immigration policy, which has trapped this young college-age population in a state of despair. Section three describes the negation of lived spaces by undocumented youth. The final section presents conclusions.

A History of Anti-Mexican Sentiment

Scholars have documented the educational plight and struggle of Mexican Americans in the United States (Acuña, 2007; Chavez, 1991; Zinn, 2003). Few, however, have examined the link between the historically unrelenting discrimination against the Mexican-origin population and American social policies, including educational policy, of the twentieth and twenty-first centuries. The examination of continual historical prejudice would appear an important resource in understanding the age-old debate of who has the right to what in the United States.

Who has the right to be in this country and who has the right to an American education? I propose that deep-seeded prejudice has always undermined the Mexican-origin community's quest for acceptance and equality in the United States. There exists a tendency in this country to ignore, discredit, and discount Mexican heritage, and schools have often

9

been a medium in disseminating this bias. The educational structure, after all, reflects the nation's dominant society's view of its self (Pizarro, 2005; Velez-Ibanez, 1996). Since the creation of the "American way of life" in the eighteenth century, the sociopolitical and cultural identification of an "American" was based on white, Protestant, Northern European male privilege. As Howard Zinn recounts in his book *A People's History of the United States:*

> The inferior position of blacks, the exclusion of Indians from the new society, the establishment of supremacy for the rich and powerful in the new nation—all this was already settled in the colonies by the time of the revolution (Zinn, 1980, p. 89).

This proposition contradicts the popular teaching of the melting pot premise in the United States and invites a discussion on cultural pluralism. In his work, *Cultural Pluralism Historical Perspective,* Mark M. Krug looks into the past to set the stage for his arguments on cultural pluralism. Krug analyzes the exclusionary concepts of "Americanization," the "Melting Pot," and "Cultural Pluralism" as frameworks created to discuss integration of the immigrant population in the United States. Krug states that "Americanization" stipulated complete assimilation to American culture and that its proponents saw education as the vehicle for rapid and successful integration of immigrant children into American society (Krug, 1971).

On the "Melting Pot" theory, Krug was of the position that its supporters saw American culture in a formative stage and as still evolving. The "Melting Pot" theorist saw the blending of immigrant and native cultures giving form and life to American culture. Critics of the "Melting Pot" saw it as dangerous and destructive to America and American culture. They pointed to Mestizaje in Mexico as producing a nation of half-breeds unable to self govern (Krug, 1971).

"Cultural Pluralism" was a theoretical and workable approach to the relations of the dominant society and ethnic European immigration groups in the United States. This theory proposed that American society was not monolithic but pluralistic (Krug, 1971). Krug believed that the driving ideology of "Cultural Pluralism" could be used to advance the causes of the non-white population. For this to happen, however, a new form of "Cultural Pluralism" had to exist, one that was more inclusive and contemporary. In its traditional proposal "Cultural Pluralism was far from "Multiculturalism" or equitable (Krug, 1971). Its pluralism was limited to Euro-Americans (Acuña, 2007; Chavez, 1991; Zinn, 2003).

Krug's work, like others, focuses primarily on European immigrants and leaves many unanswered questions about other immigrant populations such as Mexican immigrants, as well as the integration of the indigenous first nations that preceded all immigrants.

Another important area of research is the root of hate as manifested in American nativism. Such a question is vital to better identify with the historical antecedents of *de facto* and *de jure* segregation, including segregation in one of our most important American institutions, education. Moreover, the long-term impact of the educational structure was a perpetuation of social theories espousing racial differences.

Nowhere is there a more supportive argument for the contradiction of integration models in the United States than in the racist writings of Lewis M. Terman (1916) when he wrote:

> Among laboring men and servant girls there are thousands like them .... The tests have told the truth. These boys are uneducable beyond the merest rudiments of training. No amount of school instruction will ever make them intelligent voters or capable citizens .... They represent the level of intelligence which is very, very common among Spanish-Indian and Mexican families of the Southwest and also among Negroes. Their dullness seems to be racial, or at least inherent in the family stocks from which they came. The fact that one meets this type with such extraordinary frequency among Indians, Mexicans, and Negroes suggests quite forcibly that the whole question of racial differences in mental traits will have to be taken up anew and by experimental methods. The writer predicts that when this is done there will be discovered enormously significant racial differences in general intelligence, differences which cannot be wiped out by any scheme of mental culture. Children of this group should be segregated in special classes and be given instruction, which is concrete and practical. They cannot master abstractions, but they can often be made efficient workers, able to look out for themselves. There is no possibility at present of convincing society that they should not be allowed to reproduce, although from a eugenic point of view they constitute a grave problem because of their unusually prolific breeding (pp. 91–92).

Eugenics, a sort of pseudoscience, was used to rationalize and legitimize social segregation in the United States in the early twentieth century. This was especially true in schools where the arguments of deficit theory were cemented in racism. Much of the seed of racism against the Mexican-origin community had been planted centuries earlier. Indeed, to locate the roots of anti-Mexican sentiment, which continue to plague society and its institutions, we must look deep into the past.

In his work *Origins of Anti Mexican Sentiment,* Raymond A. Paredes traces the roots of the discrimination experienced by the community of Mexican ancestry in the United States. He proposes that the anti-Mexican sentiment has its roots in Europe as the product of political and religious conflict. From the conflict between Spain and England, and between the Protestant and Catholic Churches emerged powerful anti-Spanish sentiment and fear. From the pulpit and the podium, racist and anti-Catholic sentiments were spread, giving rise to what historians have labeled *Hispanophobia* and *The Black Legend* (Paredes, as cited in Ornelas, 2000).

Both Hispanophobia and The Black legend depicted a grotesque view of all things Spanish and Catholic. The Spaniards had been placed at the bottom of the Elizabethan model, as they were seen as a product of Moorish miscegenation morally corrupted by the Catholic Church and the Spanish Crown. Paredes points out that this anti-Spanish sentiment was more pronounced in America, since the English colonies were established at a time when Hispanophobia was at an all time high (Paredes, as cited in Ornelas, 2000).

This anti-Spanish and anti-Catholic sentiment transcended into an anti-Mexican sentiment, which justified horrible abuses beyond institutional racism as Old World hatred carried into the New World and the new American nations. The Mexican was seen as even worse than the Spaniard because of further mestizaje through its indigenous ancestry (Paredes, as cited in Ornelas, 2000). This prejudice toward Mestizo Catholics would play a major role in the formation and expansion of the United States.

Racism played an important part in the U.S.–Mexican War 1846–1848 and continued to be an instrument of oppression well into the present. The racism that would justify segregation, legal or otherwise, was echoed throughout the early years of Mexican and American conflict. Major William H. Emory stated in a "Report on the United States and Mexican Boundary Survey" in 1859: The "white race" was "exterminating or crushing out the inferior race" (Larralde and Jacobo, 2000, p. 25).

Others echoed his remarks. A United States soldier in the same year noted, "The Mexican, like the poor Indian, is doomed to retire before the more enterprising Anglo-Americans." Frederick Olmsted noted that Mexicans were seen "not as heretics or heathens to be converted ... but rather as vermin, to be exterminated" (Larralde and Jacobo, 2000, p. 25).

Mexicans were bitterly resented for their amalgamation or assimilation through miscegenation. Edward B. Foote wrote in his renowned, bulky medical reference book on the subject of marriage that the Mexican "population is divided between Mestizos, Mulattoes, and Zambos, many of whom are but little above the savage, go naked, have no established forms of marriage .... Those who do not associate with and imitate the customs of the whites, are omnigamic, and governed by their impulses" (Larralde and Jacobo, 2000, p. 25).

Distinguished scholars, such as Joseph Simms, who compiled a massive, celebrated college textbook that went through ten editions, often supported these racist statements. Those of Indian background, Simms wrote, had a face that "clearly betrays a degenerate nature." He stressed that "Dark races, like the Indian and Negro, are naturally revengeful, like the elephant; and black eyes evince more or less a revengeful disposition." He concluded that dark people, especially those of Indian blood, had "a wide mouth, and a narrow face, [that] may safely be defined as indicative of animal imitation" (Larralde and Jacobo, 2000, p. 25).

Since Mexicans were viewed as inferior, they were merely excluded from the human race. Their physical appearance and conduct made it possible to regard them as repulsive. In 1874 Edward King and J. Wells Champney noted how the Mexican in San Antonio could not be made to see that "his slow, primitive ways, his filth and lack of comfort, are not better than the frugal decency and careful home management of the Germans and Americans who surround him" (Larralde and Jacobo, 2000, p. 26).

This racial rhetoric dominated social and political circles well into the twentieth century, justifying segregation and violence against the Mexican community in all sectors of American society. Rodolfo Acuña (2007) quotes a congressional report in 1930, which read.

Their [the Mexicans'] minds run to nothing higher than animal functions—eat, sleep, and sexual debauchery. In every huddle of Mexican shacks one meets the same idleness, hordes of hungry dogs, and filthy children with faces plastered with flies, disease, lice, human filth, stench, promiscuous fornication, bastardy, lounging, apathetic peons and lazy squaws, beans and dried chili, liquor, general squalor, and envy and hatred of the gringo. These people sleep by day and prowl by night like coyotes, stealing anything they can get their hands on, no matter how useless to them it may be. Nothing left outside is safe unless padlocked or chained down.

Yet there are Americans clamoring for more of this human swine to be brought over from Mexico (Acuña, 2007, p. 209).

Even when foreign threats loomed, discrimination including in education, persisted against Mexicans. In 1943 at the height of the Second World War, despite Mexican American contribution to the war effort, Acuña (2007) finds an official report by the Los Angeles police department, which read:

Although the report admitted that discrimination against Chicanos in employment, education, schooling, recreation, and labor unions was common, it concluded that Chicanos were inherently criminal and violent. Ayres stated that Chicanos were Indians, that Indians were Orientals, and that Orientals had an utter disregard for life. Therefore, because Chicanos had these inborn characteristics, they were too violent. The report further alleged that Chicanos were cruel, for they descended from the Aztecs who supposedly sacrificed 30,000 victims a day! Ayres wrote that Indians considered leniency a sign of weakness, pointing to the Mexican government's treatment of the Indians, which he maintained was quick and severe. He urged that all gang members be imprisoned and that all Chicano youths over the age of 18 be given the option of working or enlisting in the armed forces. Chicanos, according to Ayres, could not change their spots; they had an innate desire to use a knife and let blood, and this inborn cruelty was aggravated by the liquor and jealousy. The Ayres report, which represented official law enforcement views, goes a long way in explaining the events around Sleepy Lagoon" (Acuña, 2007, p. 253).

It is apparent that the perception of people of Mexican origin as animal like and sub-human was reflected in all sectors of American society, including the educational structure. It is not surprising, therefore, that Mexican students who were victims of such prejudice were also agents of change in demanding educational justice and the construction of social-political spaces. Mexican-origin children and their parents were at the forefront in the struggle against segregation in American schools (Darder, Torres, and Gutaierrez, 1997).

Institutional Racism and the Mexican-American Education

A long struggle for equity in education marks the history of American schools in the Mexican-origin community. A series of court cases document this struggle for a democratic education. In 1931, the case of *Roberto Alvarez vs. the Lemon Grove School Board* in San Diego County, California, set the stage for other cases.

On January 5, 1931, Jerome T. Green, principal of the Lemon Grove Grammar School, acting on a school board decision, barred seventy-five children of Mexican descent from entering school. According to the school board and the Parent Teacher Association, these children caused health and sanitation problems, and they came from homes where ignorance and poverty prevailed. Full of cultural prejudice, the Lemon Grove School District in California secretly established a separate school for students of Mexican ancestry in the hope of "Americanizing" them (Griswold del Castillo, 2008).

Outraged that their children were being segregated from the Anglo children, the Mexican-American community of this San Diego suburb sued the Lemon Grove School Board and won. The victory was based on the premise that Mexicans were officially caucasians. State law allowed segregation only of black, Asian, and Indian children; caucasian students could not legally be segregated from other Caucasians (Griswold del Castillo, 2008).

Another important case was *Mendez vs. Westminster and the California Board of Education*. In March of 1945, Mexican parents in Orange County, California confronted the segregation of their children into "Mexican Schools" with the help of the League of United Latin American Citizens (LULAC). The Mexican parents and LULAC sued four local school districts for segregating their children (Acuña, 2007). They were victorious. This landmark case challenged segregation in California school districts and gave support to the Brown Supreme Court Decision of 1954. Governor Earl Warren signed legislation prohibiting segregation in California, giving equal rights to all students.

The Mendez case was a victory for equality in education in California (Velez-Ibanes, 1996). The national victory would come with *Brown vs. Board of Education*. In 1954, the U.S. Supreme Court ruled that compulsory segregation of races in public schools was unconstitutional. The court held that separate facilities for black and white students were "inherently unequal," and in 1955, ordered states with segregated schools to open them to all races with deliberate speed (Acuña, 2007).

The racialization and marginalization of the Mexican American in such areas as education and the return of Mexican ancestry soldiers from World War II and the Korean War provided background and impetus for the Chicano movement. This historical experience gave birth to the roots of the Chicana/o quest for civil rights in the United States as well as the creation of Chicana/o sociopolitical space. Mexican-origin people demanded equality and justice in all sectors of society, especially in education (Acuña, 2007; Chavez, 1991; Gutierrez, 1988).

The awakening of social consciousness during the sixties and seventies produced social movements and several reforms in education, including the introduction of bilingual education and the creation of Chicano Studies departments in the Southwest. The legacy of discrimination, however, continues to permeate the American landscape. It reshapes itself, taking new social political dimensions. Presently, as in the past, this includes debates over Mexican legal and illegal immigration and access to education (Acuna 2007; Chavez 1991; Gutttierez, 1988).

The current social divide over immigration policy in the United States suggests that social fragmentation and xenophobia continue to permeate American society. It is also clear that engaging in any discourse over these divisions cannot be separated from discussions on race and class in American society. In fact, race and class are at the core of the recent protest by hundreds of thousands of immigrants, their families, and their supporters (Mariscal, 2006).

In particular, walkouts by Mexican-origin youth from schools must be seen as much more than a form of protest against a failed immigration policy that targets the undocumented population in the United States. It is also an explosion of emotions against a system and ideology that continuously marginalizes and criminalizes the Mexican-origin community (Mariscal, 2006).

As we enter the twenty-first century, the economic global crisis of profit-driven markets has brought the issue of immigration policy into debate. On the one hand, there is the need for cheap labor, and, on the other, the emphasis is on the issue of controlling the borders of the nation (Gaona, 2006).

Dependency on Mexican Labor and a Failed Immigration Policy

It is a federal crime to enter the United States without legal authorization. Many, if not the vast majority of the students, who are in the United States illegally, however, did not make the personal choice to enter illicitly into the country. No one knows the exact facts, but it is safe to state that most of these youth crossed the border illegally as young children. Their parents—some legal, some not—were hopeful that immigration reform would one day take place, regularizing their family's legal status in the United States. Unfortunately, in an attempt to keep their families together, these parents place their children in a perilous and uncertain predicament.

Not all responsibility, however, should fall on the parents. I propose that accountability also rest on the historical dependency on Mexican labor in this country and in the failures of our federal immigration policies. In particular the absence of a viable and just immigration policy that meets the labor demands of the nation while keeping immigrants and their families together.

Regrettably, immigration and, in particular, illegal immigration, especially from Mexico, is rarely seen as a human and humane issue in the United States. More often it is associated only with the economic cost of benefits to illegal aliens. It is also safe to say that, for most Americans, the immigration debate is held in a contemporary capsule. It is seen as a current problem. Legal and illegal immigration from Mexico to the United States, however, has been ongoing for over one hundred years, and it has often been triggered by American demand for inexpensive labor (Acuña, 2007).

In addition, most Americans see immigration as one-dimensional in terms of its causes and take no responsibility for its existence. This again, is particularly true of undocumented immigration. Few people are aware of historical immigration patterns established by the demand of American labor markets. Fewer take responsibility as consumers for its existence (Balderrama and Rodriguez, 1995).

Migration is often contextualized as patterns governed by push and pull factors which activate population relocation. Simply stated, the push factors are those that are driving people out of the country of origin. They can be subdivided into social, political, and economic factors, with unemployment, war, and repression often at the head of the list (Acuña, 2007).

The pull factor, on the other hand, is the force that pulls people into a place. This is often associated with employment opportunities, freedoms, or what Mexican and Central American immigrants simply call "una vida mejor," a better life. The idea and ideal of "una vida mejor" is found continuously in the narratives in the general immigrant voice (Jacobo, 2006).

The historically consistent dominating pull factor has been an American economic vortex. The formal and informal American economy and, in particular, its labor-intensive sectors have historically fed on the inexpensive labor pool south of the border. The pull factor can be developing economic spaces, unenforced immigration policy, and the general American standard of living. From the chicken farms of the Midwest to the *maquiladoras* (factories of selected products) in California to maintenance of neighborhood lawns are examples of the pull factor in effect (Acuña, 2007).

Nevertheless, it is simplistic to address these push and pull factors of migration patterns. A host of conditions and challenges, as well as a range of emotions, marks the exodus of millions of people around the world. Behind are left loved ones, homes, and the battered dreams and aspirations of entire populations. Perhaps that is the reason that, despite the years in economic exile, Mexicans in the United States still see Mexico as home (Jacobo, 2006).

A brief examination of immigration policy in the twentieth century can attest to America's appetite for Mexican labor and its dire consequences. Simply put, historical demand for inexpensive goods and services, as well as corporate desire for increased profits, has created an economic vortex which functions as a lure for immigrants, both legal and illegal, from across the border (Balderrama and Rodriguez, 1995).

The United States, however, has historically failed in implementing practical and viable immigration laws that regulate the legal status of immigrant populations and their families. As a result the country has always had serious problem with families who have members, especially children, illegally in the country (Dardel et al., 1997).

The interdependency between Mexican labor and American industry began late in the eighteen hundreds as the American Southwest was transformed from a local plaza economy to a national and international market. It should be pointed out that industrialization highlighted by the railroad system facilitated such a transition. This is also true of land reclamation acts that transformed deserts into agriculturally productive areas. Three industries experienced unparalleled growth: mining, agribusiness, and transportation (Acuña, 2007). All three would depend heavily on Mexican labor.

Accompanying the development of these industries were changes to traditional labor in the form of anti-Asian immigration policy, such as the Chinese Exclusion Act of 1882 and the Gentleman's Act of 1907. The Gentleman's Act curtailed Japanese immigration. The curtailing of Asian immigration was to have a direct impact on Mexican immigration, as Mexico would become a labor pool for many American industries. Those industries became more and more dependent on Mexican labor throughout the twentieth century (Acuña, 2007).

Mexican labor was very appealing. What made it so attractive was its cost and the presence of skilled and unskilled labor. Availability was also an important attraction, as Mexican labor was easily accessible and easily discarded. This dependency on Mexican labor, cemented in the late eighteen hundreds, can be seen in a number of programs, laws, and social environments existing early in the twentieth century, such as the Enganche System, the 1917 Immigration Law, and the Bracero Program (Gutierrez, 1998).

The mining companies of Arizona are a clear example of this early dependence on Mexican labor, as they engaged in what was known as the *Enganche* system. The Enganche system was a form of direct recruitment by American mining companies. Mining companies in southern Arizona were aware of skilled Mexican miners and send Enganchadores to hook the Mexican workers by offering them jobs in the Arizona mines. The hiring of Mexicans to work in the United States through this system was in violation of American law, but it rarely led to criminal charges. The profits to be made were too great (Balderama and Rodriguez, 1995).

Mexican families were lured by the possibility of employment and attracted by the dollar. What they encountered, however, was exploitation, segregation, and hostility. Mexican workers were paid half the wages of white workers and given the most dangerous and undesirable jobs in the industry. This occupational segregation was accompanied by social segregation that divided the towns and services by race. It was clear that while the Mexican-origin population was vital to the economic interest of the region, their presence was also seen as a social threat. Schools were not safe from racism, and segregated schools for Mexican-origin children were common in the southwest during this period (Darder et al., 1997, Acuña, 2007).

The lack of enforcement or the tailoring of immigration laws by the American government throughout the twentieth century also indicates the historic addiction to Mexican labor. A clear example of this is the 1917 immigration law. The 1917 immigration law placed taxation and a literacy exam on "appropriate" immigrant populations (Gutierrez, 1988).

Due to pressure from corporations, the law was temporarily not enforced on Mexicans. Some scholars believe that the law was suspended for the duration of World War I because enforcing the law on Mexicans would have had a negative effect on America's operations during the war (Acuña, 2007). As with the Enganche Program, the Mexican-origin population faced blatant discrimination and schools were often the vehicles by which discrimination was disseminated.

However, no law or program reflects the reliance on Mexican labor and its social consequences more than the Bracero Program in the '40s '50s and '60s. The Bracero Program began as demands for labor increased in the United States once the country had been catapulted into the Second World War. The demand was especially high in the agricultural and railroad industry.

Faced with a labor shortage, farmers quickly turned toward Mexico, demonstrating a continuing pattern of dependency on Mexican labor by agribusiness and other sectors in the United States that had existed prior to the war. The Bracero Program was conceived of as an emergency wartime measure, but it was renewed after the war and continued until 1964, providing a huge stimulus for Mexican immigration to the United States. During the Bracero Program, almost five million Mexican workers came to the United States (Jacobo, 2000).

The program had various consequences on the struggle for civil rights. One effect was that it increased the numbers of Mexicans who came to live in the United States since many Braceros did not go back to Mexico and many more crossed into the U.S. without documents because of the unmet demand for farm laborers.

The Bracero Program, however, also perpetuated discrimination and exploitation. Bracero camps were segregated from whites and even from the Mexican-American sections of town. Braceros lived in extreme poverty and worked in dangerous conditions. When they ventured outside the camps on weekends, they frequently were the victims of racially inspired beatings and robberies (Gutierrez, 1998; Jacobo, 2000).

Some scholars suggest that the Bracero Program established the contours of modern Mexican immigration flows and gave rise to the social, political, and cultural issues that dominate discourse over immigration in the present (Jacobo, 2000). As stated, many Braceros stayed in the United States illegally at the end of the program. They eventually brought their families, hoping that one day the immigration laws would change.

More recently, the Amnesty Act of 1986, known as the Immigration Reform and Control Act of 1986 (IRCA), not only proved the need to secure foreign labor, but also created much of the turmoil we are currently experiencing in the last decade of the 20th century. The law granted amnesty to undocumented immigrants who entered the U.S before January 1, 1982, and resided here. While the law placed some two million people on a path to citizenship, it did little to rapidly unite families, thus creating a wave of children entering the United States illegally. These children eventually went to school and were the target of Proposition 187 in California (Acuña, 2007).

Proposition 187 was a controversial but popular proposition that passed in 1994 by 58.8 percent of the vote. Its goal was to bar illegal immigrants from receiving social services, health care, and public education, under the SAVE OUR STATE initiative. Persons wishing to receive public benefits had to prove their legal immigration status. It allowed law enforcement to investigate the legal status of anyone suspected of being illegal in the country. The law was overturned by federal courts, but not without adding to the legacy of anti-immigrant sentiment in the United States (Acuña, 2007).

The Amnesty Act also made it illegal to hire or recruit undocumented immigrants, thus making it a crime to hire illegal immigrants and allowing discrimination, especially toward Latinos, to increase. Legal Latinos had to settle for lower wages and worse working conditions. The act was highly criticized for not solving the immigration problem. Many critics use it as proof that amnesty agendas do not solve the problem, since the illegal immigrant population has increased since its passage in 1986 (Acuña, 2007).

All these programs and laws react to labor demands in the United States, but no serious and concrete effort has been made to regulate the status of undocumented workers and to provide for reunification with their families. Thus, the consequence is the influx of undocumented children to the United States to be with their families with the hope that one day the laws will change.

When undocumented children enter school, they face a world of uncertainty and fear. At a very young age they must confront the reality that they are illegally in the United States and could very well be detained and deported. The separation of families is a real and common occurrence in the United States. For many of these children, however, years can go by without ever being detained. Nevertheless, they consistently struggle with having to negotiate their lived spaces. They live shadowed lives.

The Negotiation of Lived Spaces: Undocumented in American Schools

People of Mexican ancestry in the United States are able to render testimony on discrimination and marginalization in this country. The Mexican-origin population in the United States has long been engaged in a struggle for justice and the creation of social, political, and cultural space. Being illegal in the United States, however, adds a whole new dimension to this struggle, particularly in the formative years of one's life. Regrettably, despite its enormous need, there is scant literature on this subject and a need to contribute to this important but neglected area of study (Acuña, 2007; Chavez, 1991; Soja, 1996;).

In his work, *Third Space: Journeys to Los Angeles and Other Real-and-Imagined Places,* Edward W. Soja (1996) stipulates that "an increasing realization of the interwoven complexity of the historical, social, and spatial realms; their inseparability and their interdependence is taking place" (p. 3). Historical and contemporary consciousness is certainly vital in the study of the struggle for cultural and social space. This would emerge to be true also in the discourse over the negotiation of lived space—living undocumented in rural and urban communities of the nation.

At the center of this social consciousness is the idea that human beings are essentially spatial beings. Spatiality in this discourse is inclusive of beliefs, events, and manifestation, as well as value. As such, this pose becomes central not only in the study of the Chicana/o struggle for cultural space in the United States, but of undocumented youth and their negotiation of lived spaces. How American society sees these undocumented youth and how these youth see themselves is a fundamental question.

Consistently, having to create frameworks in order to define oneself propels one to the creation of third spaces. For renowned scholar David G. Gutierrez (2008), this created "third space" is the place where historically Mexicans in the United States, have "attempted to mediate the profound sense of displacement" as they struggled with the racialization and marginalization of their culture.

The negotiation and creation of a third space in the Mexican-origin community presents the opportunity for one to create a framework to study the negotiation of lived spaces by unauthorized youth by adding the variable of legal status. While it may sound simple, the fact is that a major traumatic element is being added to the dimensions of how youth deal with uncertainty, both explicitly and implicitly.

While there are limited studies on this population, data suggest that undocumented youth are particularly under severe psychological strain. They suffer from extreme isolation, are vulnerable, and are easily exploited (Strong and Meiners, 2007). Undocumented students tend to live in fear and shame, feelings that are often fueled by political discourse and biased media in the United States. Current activity by immigration law enforcement of raiding low-income communities looking for undocumented persons has raised concerns by human rights groups and immigration reform activist (Acuña, 2007).

A recent study commissioned by The National Council of La Raza (NCLR) and conducted by the Urban Institute highlights the trauma experienced by children who have been affected by operations conducted by the U.S. Immigration and Customs Enforcement (ICE). ICE is the interior enforcement arm of the Department of Homeland Security, and in recent years the agency has multiplied its efforts in the deportation of the unauthorized population (Capps, Castaneda, Chudry, and Santos, 2007).

The operations have galvanized debates over accountability of child welfare, as ICE raids have resulted in the separation of hundreds of children from their parents. According to the report, a majority of these children are American citizens and make up the youngest and most vulnerable of our population—infants, toddlers and preschoolers. Moreover, the data suggest that millions of children could face the peril of being separated from their parents. It is estimated that some five million children born in the United States have at least one undocumented parent (Capps et al., 2007).

The study titled "The Impact of Immigration Raids on America's Children" documents the short- and long-term impact on the immigrant children population as a result of the separation from their parents. Immediate concerns include lack of supervision as well as and lack of basic necessities, such as food, baby formula, diapers, and clothing. The separation of the family is, without a doubt, a central concern. Such has become the fear of these raids that cases have been documented of families hiding in the basement or closets of their homes for days and sometimes weeks (Capps et al., 2007).

Furthermore, the article "The Impact of Immigration Raids on America's Children" postulates that long-term impact was experienced in "difficulty coping with the economic and psychological stress caused by the arrest and the uncertainty of not knowing when or if the arrested parent would be released" (Capps et al., 2007 p. 3). In general, children experienced symptoms of emotional trauma, such as fear, feelings of abandonment, isolation, depression, separation-anxiety, and other forms of post-traumatic stress disorder (Capps et al., 2007).

Post-Traumatic Stress Disorder (PTSD) has historically been viewed as a psychological condition belonging generally within the domain of traumatized military veterans and those who have experienced the horrors of genocide and sexual abuse. However, such views of PSTD are currently seen as partial, and the identification of PSTD is consistently been expanded.

Post-Traumatic Stress Disorder is generally defined as an anxiety disorder that can develop after exposure to a terrifying event or ordeal in which grave physical harm occurred or was threatened. Moreover, traumatic events that may trigger PTSD include violent personal assaults, natural or human-caused disasters, accidents, and military combat (Plotnik, 2005).

The National Institute of Public Health and the Diagnostic and Statistical Manual of Mental Disorders are cited when defining a victim of PTSD as (1) the person (who) experienced, witnessed, or was confronted with an event or events that involved actual or threatened death or serious injury, or a threat to the physical integrity of self or others. (2) The person's (victim's) response involved intense fear, helplessness, or horror (Behavenet, 2000).

Given these classifications, the parameters of PTSD to the unauthorized population experience is not farfetched. The daily life of an unauthorized person is one of perpetual fear, stress, physical hardship, and often traumatic physical abuse. Often, in fact, these traumas can be reproduced internally in the family in the form of domestic violence. Most undocumented people live in fear of detection and subsequent deportation. Thus, most endure violence, near subsistence wages, unsafe working environments, and unsanitary working and living conditions (Acuña, 2007; Diaz et al., 2007).

Most undocumented people avoid public safety institutions and police, and hence often are the victims of harassment, theft, assault, domestic abuse, and frequently, rape (Chavez, 1991). There exists a pervasive sense that the unauthorized population has no voice, no say, and no rights. These are feelings that resonate deep and influence the negotiation of lived spaces of the unauthorized population in the United States.

It should be noted that the report by the Urban Institute commissioned by National Council of La Raza focuses primarily on United States citizens whose parents are in the country unauthorized. While the report does acknowledge that as many as a third of the children affected by the raids are in the country illegally, the research alludes to the fact that it does not examine the trauma experienced by unauthorized youth (Capps et al., 2007). There exists a major void in the research when the issues of unauthorized youth in the United States are concerned; this is particularly true of those pursuing a college education.

The recent failures of immigration reform, including the Dream Act of 2003, further alienated this young population, as their legal and academic status continues to be unresolved. The Dream Act was proposed through federal legislation that was designed to grant high school students with good academic standing legal status in the United States. Legal status would also be extended to undocumented immigrants of good moral character who wanted to serve in the armed forces or attend college. Given the political environment created by the 2008 elections, the Dream Act was derailed (Jefferies, 2007).

From a developmental age perspective, the psychological stress experienced by undocumented youth builds up as they enter high school and college. At a critical time in their lives they are conditioned and restrained by their legal status in the United States. Access to higher education for undocumented students is a highly contested issue, and federal and state governments have attempted to address it with little success.

Several states including California, Utah, New York, Oklahoma, Washington, Kansas, Illinois, New Mexico, and Nebraska have passed legislation which allows undocumented students who have graduated from state high schools to pay in-state tuition (Jefferies, 2007).

In California, Assembly Bill 540 of 2001 allows immigrant students to pay in-state tuition if they meet a host of requirements. To qualify a student must have attended a California high school for three or more years. Students must have a California high school diploma or GED. They must sign a statement with the school, stating that he/she will apply for legal residency as soon as they are eligible to do so. Through this bill, undocumented students can register or be enrolled in California Community College, California State University, or the University of California campuses. This has created uproar in many American communities who see such laws as pandering to illegal aliens (Jefferies, 2007).

In some states unauthorized students are able to attend college and pay in-state tuition, but cannot receive any economic assistance. They are unintentionally limited to certain majors, which would not require them to reveal their legal status. For instance, international business majors are required to study abroad. Moreover, when they complete their education they cannot legally work in the United States. Simply put, they are in a quagmire which positions these youth in a constant negotiation of their lived spaces as youth, students, and illegal aliens.

The legal and political conditions have catapulted these youth into an arena where they have to consistently negotiate the tensions produced by their official status. Their world is demarcated by incompatible legal parameters some denoting regulated social policy while others are evidently creating spaces were unregulated social policy exist (Vock, 2008). This legal dimension of immigration social policy is expressed from a legal continuum—at one end is unauthorized and unregulated social spaces and at the other end unauthorized but regulated social spaces.

As such unauthorized youth have to consistently negotiate their lived spaces. One moment they may be gifted college students in an unregulated legal space (college campus) and the very next they are committing a federal crime by being in the United States unauthorized (outside of the college campus).

Given these tensions, a dimension of lived space is produced. The lived space dimension is expressed as *explicit lived space and implicit lived space*. The explicit lived space is what the individual is willing to share or is known to him/her and others. The implicit lived space is what the individual is not willing to share with others that s/he interacts with. The fear of disclosing information of legal status or been exposed creates such traumas as those defined in the operational definitions of this work (Merton, 1957).

It should be noted that research on this subject is most critical for the geographical area of Southern California. Proximity to the United States Mexico border cannot be discounted as an influential factor. The politics and antipolitics in the immigration debate take center stage in many of the border cities such as San Diego California (Jacobo et al., 2004).

Depending on one's political beliefs or one's needs, the border denotes different things for different people. For some, the U.S/Mexican border is a transgression against humanity while others sleep better at night because of its existence. Since the implementation of "Operation Gatekeeper" in 1994, the Southern California border has become a barrier to life itself, claiming the lives of some five thousand immigrants—woman, men, and children (Jacobo et al., 2004).

The U.S.–Mexico Border in the San Diego/Tijuana sector is demarcated by a wall made of rusting Vietnam era aircraft landing plates, salvaged by local Republican representatives in Congress, and welded into place by the United States Navy Seabees and the Army Corps of Engineers. The wall extends west from the industrial parks of Otay Mesa and descends into the Pacific Ocean (Jacobo, Flores, and Correa, 2004).

San Diego has always been a politically conservative city and it has witnessed its share of anti-immigrant sentiments. These sentiments have been expressed in a variety of ways, from the activities of the Ku Klux Klan in the early part of the twentieth century to overwhelming support for California propositions like 228, the English only initiative, and the controversial Proposition 187, calling for the denial of social and health services to undocumented persons. In the early twenty-first century, the patrolling of places of hire, such as Home Depot, and barrios by the Minutemen have added tension (Acuna, 2007; Jacobo et al., 2004).

We can posit that tensions over the immigration debate are higher in border cities, as these are perceived by the anti-immigrant faction as the frontline against what they perceive is an invasion taking place through unauthorized entry into the United States. Groups like the Minutemen operate under a creed that stipulates complete dominion over American borders. Given these tensions, one can also deduce that the trauma experienced by the unauthorized population grows higher as they are consistently harassed and threatened (Acuña, 2007).

Trauma is a psychological distressing experience outside the range of common human experience. It can occur as the result of months or years of abuse or neglect, or in the wake of a single overwhelming event. Trauma often involves a sense of fear, terror, and helplessness in the face of a real or a perceived threat to one's self or a loved one's well being (Perry, 2006). Apprehension, deportation, and family separation by immigration authorities can generate such conditions. Proximity to the U.S.–Mexico border creates an environment where traumatic conditions can flourish (Capps et al., 2007).

Trauma is an experience that induces an abnormally intense and prolonged stress response. Trauma overwhelms a person's ability to cope. This is more so in young people and children. Common effects or conditions that may occur include physical, emotional, and cognitive responses such as sleep disturbances, depression, anxiety, distraction, avoidance, and hyper vigilance (Capps et al., 2007; Perry, 2006).

As addressed earlier in this review, post-traumatic stress disorder can also be a stress response to trauma that can occur in some people after experiencing trauma. In short, historical prejudice, the American appetite for inexpensive labor, and an unviable immigration policy have produced an array of problems. One of the major problems produced is the criminalization and virtual incarceration of unauthorized youth. The heated debate, the failure of immigration reform, and in particular the stalling of the Dream Act in the mid-2000s have left these youth in a state of confusion, despair, and uncertainty.

Conclusion

The issue of higher education for undocumented high school graduates has increasingly gained notice in the United States. Several states have passed laws to give these students access to college at in-state tuition rates, but Federal regulations limit their access to financial aid. Education and immigration advocates, as well as immigrant students, are pushing to widen the access to public colleges and universities nationwide (Jefferies, 2007; Vock, 2008).

Efforts to change discriminatory laws and regulations controlling access to higher education are not without resistance. Opposition often fueled by blatant discrimination is widespread. Immigrants face increasing attacks by governmental legislation and enforcement. As in the past, people hold immigrants responsible for economic woes in the U.S. (Acuña, 2007; Bingham, 2003).

There is, however, some hope. While published works on this topic are limited, there are scholars who are beginning to shed light on this issue. Scholar Alejandra Rincon (2009) has recently put together a book on the subject entitled *"Undocumented Immigrants and Higher Education."* In addition Dr. William Perez at Claremont Graduate University is conducting studies on strategies for supporting community-college high-achieving undocumented students. Moreover, several theses and dissertations in some way relate to the subject, are currently being written.

This work will add an important human dimension to the discourse over undocumented youth in education. Through the use of case studies, the human condition of this reality needs to be analyzed. This study investigates the negotiation of lived spaces by unauthorized students at community colleges/CSU campuses in Southern California. These students are part of a larger unknown nationwide community that is thriving in spite of the constraints society has place on them. They are young people full of dreams and hopes, despite their criminalization and virtual internment in the United States.

In the next few chapters, the methodology used for the study and case studies begin to document the personal trauma experienced by college-aged unauthorized students and to underscore the importance of addressing this neglected issue. When doing so, historical prejudice and the failure of immigration policy that condemns youth into a lifetime of uncertainty must be addressed. Chapter four begins with the researcher's own reflections of unauthorized lived spaces in order to further establish the social context of this study.

Methodology

This chapter provides an overview of the methodology that frames the qualitative multi-case study approach of the study. A qualitative case study narrative approach was used to document the voices of undocumented college-age youth. The qualitative approach provided participants the opportunity to tell about how they have "negotiated lived space" while engaging them in dialogue on their own living conditions while being legally unauthorized to reside in the United States, in their own language (Kemmis and Wilkinson, 1998).

The chapter begins with a brief overview of the context of the study, proceeds with the research questions, conceptual framework guiding the study, approach and qualitative research methods used, how participants were selected, the procedures used in the study, participant profiles, data collection approach, and data analysis.

Context of the Study

The study focused on immigrant college-age students who are undocumented and live and attend a college in Southern California. Over two million undocumented children are enrolled in schools in the United States. The existing federal law established by the Supreme Court case *Plyler vs. Doe* in 1982 gives these children the right to a K–12 education under the Fourteenth Amendment. The court, however, never extended that right to higher levels of education (Horwedel, 2006). For the most part, the students in this study were brought to the United States by their parents who were looking for better living conditions. Over 50,000 such students are estimated to be attending a higher education institution (Horwedel, 2006). The Southern California region is the most highly impacted region in the nation with undocumented persons, specifically of Mexican ancestry (Acuña, 2007; Griswold, 2008).

Research Questions

The main question of the study was: What are the existing social-psychological forces that shape the daily-lived experiences and negotiated spaces of unauthorized youth, in particular, those pursuing access to higher levels of education in the United States?

To answer the main research question, three sub-questions were addressed:

- What are the types of daily-lived situations that confront undocumented youth sense of identity and belonging?
- What types of psychological trauma impacts how undocumented youth negotiate their daily-lived situations?
- How do Latino undocumented youth respond to the daily psychological trauma that they experience?

Conceptual Framework

The conceptual framework that guided the study seeks to analyze explicit and implicit lived spaces of unauthorized Latino youth living in the United States and how the tensions of not residing legally in the immediate and broader spaces of the community, state, and nation are negotiated.

The psychological stress experienced by undocumented youth builds up as they enter high school and college age. At a critical time in their lives, they are conditioned and restrained by their legal status in the United States. Access to higher education for undocumented students is a highly contested issue, and federal and state governments have attempted to address it with little success.

The framework used in the study consists of two dimensions. The first consists of explicit and implicit modes of behavior—behaviors that are seen by others who interact with the individual (explicit) and behaviors that are not see by others (implicit). The second dimension is the legal status of the individual or the unauthorized status of interacting and living in the United States.

The legal dimension is expressed from a legal continuum—at one end are unauthorized and unregulated social policies whereby the individual is able to negotiate his/her lived space by being very familiar with his/her surroundings. At the other end are unauthorized and regulated social policies, whereby the individual in public spaces runs the risk of being apprehended for not having legal documentation.

The socio-psychological lived space dimension is expressed as *explicit* lived space and *implicit* lived space. The explicit lived space is what the

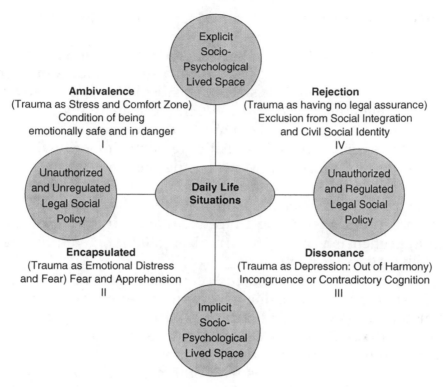

Figure 3.1 Conceptual framework for understanding the socio-psychology of lived spaces and regulated social policy in residing in the United States

individual is willing to share or is known to him/her and others. The implicit lived space is what the individual is not willing to share with others that s/he interacts with.

In the case of undocumented youth/students living in the U.S., the frameworks offers four quadrants of analysis. In the first quadrant (unauthorized and unregulated legal social policy and explicit lived space), the undocumented youth experiences ambivalence. This state of ambivalence is defined as experiencing trauma as stress while controlling his/her comfort zone.

Ambivalence is also a state of living in a part of the community where he/she feels familiar and has a high degree of awareness of civic behavior, while understanding his/her legal status and while interacting in low-risk social activities that are part of the daily social dynamics of the community. S/he, while experiencing a sense of "zone of comfort" in the community, nevertheless, has the constant worry or trauma of not being "legal" and living under stress. Involvement in activities such as church functions or family gatherings at a park are enjoyed but not without the fear of legal ramifications.

In the second quadrant (unauthorized and unregulated legal social policy and implicit socio-psychological lived space), the undocumented youth experiences encapsulation. This state of encapsulation is defined as trauma experience by emotional distress and fear. Encapsulation is illustrated as a state of constant fear known only to him/her or intimate others.

The youth is constantly aware that s/he is outside of his/her immediate community and must always be on the lookout and negotiating the lived spaces that offer him/her a sense of control. Teachers and peers are unaware of a student's legal status in an implicit lived space. Therefore, a school field trip designed to be educational and fun can elicit feelings of fear and apprehension in the unauthorized student, given that legal and disclosure barriers may be present.

In Quadrant III (unauthorized and regulated legal social policy and implicit lived space), the undocumented youth experiences dissonance. This state of dissonance is defined as trauma experienced as depression and out of harmony with surroundings. Dissonance thus is a state of living in trauma and out of harmony within the broader community and within the self. The inability to share the legal status with others creates conflict, a feeling of helplessness, and distance. A simple college night out with friends to local establishments that require a driver's license for identification becomes an emotional test for unauthorized individuals.

In Quadrant IV (unauthorized and regulated legal social policy and explicit lived space), the undocumented youth experiences rejection. This state of rejection is defined as trauma experienced through social exclusion. Rejection is also a state of living outside of the community where he/she feels excluded from civic participation. In this quadrant, the individual suffers the trauma of having no legal assurance and exclusion from social integration and civil social identity. Not being able to take part of the political process through their voice and through the voting process serves as an example of such exclusion from social and civic integration.

Using the above-described conceptual framework, the study sought to examine the existing socio-psychological forces that shape the daily-lived experiences and negotiated spaces of unauthorized youth, in particular, those pursuing access to higher levels of education in the United States. The conceptual framework serves as a tool for understanding the lived spaces and trauma experienced by unauthorized youth in the United States.

The framework allows one to analyze how unauthorized students navigate from an explicit to an implicit lived space and from a regulated to an unregulated legal space. The framework suggests a way for measuring variance in social integration. Moreover, it reveals the possible types of trauma experienced, such as feeling unsafe, stress and depression, constant emotional distress, and having no sense of civic identity and legal assurance.

Approach

Table 3.1 illustrates the interrelationship among research questions, conceptual focus, and approach used to collect data for each question of participants involved in the study.

QUESTION	CONCEPTUAL FOCUS	APPROACH
1 Daily lived situations	Lived Spaces Situations	Semi-structured interviews
2 Psychological Trauma	Types of Psychological Trauma and Coping Skills	Autobiography
3 Responses to Psychological Trauma	Negotiates Lived Behavior Response	Series of face to face meetings to follow-up on narratives to ascertain their lived situations profile
Questions 1,2, 3	Unauthorized college age students live experiences in Southern California	Case study of eight (8) college age students—four males and four females

Table 3.1 Questions, Conceptual Focus, and Approach

Qualitative Research Method

The use of qualitative methods proposes an epistemological commitment to a human-centered approach that is used to gain insight into people's attitudes, behaviors, values, concerns, motivations, aspirations, and culture or lifestyles. It is, in a sense, the study of people in their normal environment. The methodology requires that the researcher understand how individuals interpret and ascribe meaning to the world around.

An important implication of this approach is that at some level all knowledge is interpretative and hence depends on social context. Additionally, at the center of this approach rests the premise that knowledge is also shaped by the values and experience of the researcher (Blackstone, 2008; Denzin and Lincoln, 1994).

Qualitative research is a multidisciplinary field of inquiry with an array of methods, such as interactive interviewing, observation, and written descriptions. The very word *qualitative* implies a focus on "qualities of entities and on a process of meaning that are not experimentally examined of measured in terms of quantity, amount, intensity, or frequency" (Denzin and Lincoln, p. 10). At the same time, however, it does not merely imply a non-numerical response to an open-ended question.

This study used the research strategy of narrative inquiry (Connelly and Clandinin, 1994) that informs the design and implementation of the study. Narrative inquiry strives for meaning and insight on the basis of a story constructed collaboratively out of lives and experiences of both the researcher and participant. Connelly and Clandinin (1994) argue that "people live stories, and in telling them reaffirm them, modify them, and created new ones. Stories educate the self and the others" (p. 415).

The reconstructed lived stories offer a means for the participants to make sense of their experiences. In the case of the selected participants of this study, unauthorized immigrant college-age students, the construction of their stories enable previously silenced voices to find expression and validation in a "mainstream" medium (Denzin and Lincoln, 1994).

Carl F. Auerbach, proposes that "The qualitative research paradigm assumes that the best way to learn about people's subjective experience is to ask them about it, and listen carefully to what they have to say. People almost always talk about their experience in story form" (Auerbach, 2003, p. X). Thus, it is essential for the researcher to offer the participant space to navigate topics.

Such an approach is a vital part of grounded theory, which seeks to create theory. Ground theory involves gathering and examining data to construct theoretical frameworks that explain the data collected (Denzin and Lincoln, 1994). For Kathy Charmaz (as cited in Denzin and Lincoln, 2005), the term *grounded theory* refers both to a method of inquiry and to a product of inquiry.

Furthermore, according to Charmaz (Denzin and Lincoln 2005), one of the strengths of grounded theory methods is that it offers tools for analyzing processes, and these tools hold much potential for social justice issues such as the criminalization of unauthorized youth (Denzin and Linclon, 2005, p. 508). In this research study, unauthorized college-age students provided through life stories information that could not easily be quantified in by numerical measures. Moreover, there is a call for social justice for the broader community and institutions to recognize and validate their voices.

Specific Qualitative Methods

Three qualitative methods were used to collect data on each of the eight selected college-aged participants and examine the main question and three sub-questions of the study. These methods were semi-structured interviews, autobiographies, and a series of follow-up personal meetings to ascertain the lived conditions and daily negotiations of the college-age students.

These three qualitative research methods were selected for this study as the best approach to capturing how unauthorized youth make sense of their lives and their experiences, as well as their overall view of the world around them.

The data collected through the three qualitative methods was used to form the case studies of the selected participants. Case study methodology was utilized to document the lived experiences of unauthorized youth based on the interviews, autobiographies, and face-to-face meetings. Case studies produced more in-depth, comprehensive information. It employed subjective information and participant observation to describe the context, or natural setting, of the variables under consideration, as well as the interactions of the different variables in the context. Case studies were used to obtain a wide understanding of the entire lived conditions and situations experienced by undocumented youth in the study. For some scholars like Robert E. Stake, case study is not a methodological choice but a choice of what is to be studied (Denzin and Lincoln, 2005).

Selection of Participants

The selection process of eight participants involved the recruitment and identification of potential participants, invitation to participate, and the actual selection of participants. Underlying the whole study was the security and privacy guarantees of participant data, given the sensitivity of the subject. The selected college students were provided anonymity, and, throughout the process, approval had to be given before the written case studies were completed. At any time the participant had the option to deselect themselves as participants from the study.

Recruitment of participants involved two main steps. First, for participants to be involved in the study they needed to meet the following criteria:

1. Latino/a bilingual, bicultural, and bi-literate college-age students
2. Latino/a college-age youth attending a two-year or four-year college or university in Southern California

3. Lived in the United States as undocumented residents for at least twelve years
4. The participants had not received authorized legal residency in the United States.
5. Background being of Mexican ancestry

Second, to identify a pool of participants that met the four criteria, the researcher undertook the following steps:

1. Flyers were posted at local community colleges and universities in Southern California, where the researcher's phone number, e-mail address, and the purpose of the study were noted. Willing participants contacted the researcher at their convenience.
2. Once contact was established the researcher read to the willing participant the recruitment script. If a caller agreed to participate, the researcher then read the informed consent form to the caller (APPENDIX A).
3. Once it was ascertained that the caller met the study's criteria and fully understood and agreed to the informed-consent form, a one-on-one meeting was arraigned at a location of the participant's choosing. If a caller fit the criteria, the caller was immediately assigned a pseudonym of their choosing, and either their phone number or e-mail address was assigned as the method of future communication, thus protecting the participant's confidentiality and privacy.
4. If a caller did not fit the criteria, no information was documented, and there was no further contact with the caller.

Step three yielded a list of thirty-six possible participants from Southern California colleges. The invitation to participate in the study involved conversations with the thirty-six identified candidates for the study. From the list of thirty-six participants, sixteen who were of Mexican ancestry were selected, eight females and eight males who met all the five criteria previously stated. In his personal communication with the sixteen preliminary list of candidates, the researcher introduced himself as a Chicana/o Studies professor who is enrolled in a doctoral program and conducting research on unauthorized college-aged students to document their daily-lived situations and perceived struggles. Their participation would consist of a face-to-face structured interview, after which they would be guided to develop an autobiography of their life experiences, with a follow-up face-to-face meeting interview, to ascertain their lived situation, using a case study approach.

Over a one-month period, sixteen personal contacts were made, and the study was explained to the potential participants, while addressing their concerns on the sensitivity of the study and while assuring them that at any time they could deselect themselves from participating. The researcher met with each candidate at his or her local campus and at a designated time that was convenient to them.

If they affirmed their willingness to participate, they were asked to sign a written consent form targeted at a reading level between sixth and eighth grade. Another purpose of the initial meetings served two purposes: to establish trust and their willingness to participate in the study and to determine if they were willing to talk about their lives and experiences openly. The offering of confidentiality and respect of privacy was stressed to the candidates.

The selection of participants for the study was based on profiles developed during the sixteen personal meetings with candidates who met the criteria of study. From the initial sixteen profiles of candidates for the study, eight candidates were selected based on their willingness to participate and to sign a consent form giving permission to use their lived experiences, while assuring confidentiality (see Appendix A). It should be noted that by IRB regulations the students were given the choice to not sign the form, given the nature of the study. An overview of the study was provided to them to read (see Appendix B). They were asked to read all related information before giving their consent to volunteer to participate.

The eight participants consisted of four females and four males. The purpose of the study was explained to all of them: to raise consciousness on their lived experiences and the injustices experienced throughout their lives—with the intent to propose a more humane immigration policy and promote a policy that supported access to higher education. In early fall of 2009, a schedule of appointments with the eight participants was secured over a two-week period. Each initial meeting lasted between sixty to ninety minutes.

Procedures

The initial phase of the study was a series of semi-structured interviews with each respective participant. Semi-structured interviews were used since they are less intrusive to those being interviewed, as the semi-structured interview encourages two-way communication. Those being interviewed can ask questions of the interviewer.

In this way the semi-structured interview can also function as an extension tool. The semi-structured interviews did not only provide answers to questions, but the reasons for the answers. Semi-structured interviews were conducted with fairly open guidelines to allow for focused, conversational, two-way communication. The approach was used both to give and receive information. The semi-structured interviews provided general information relevant to specific issues (e.g., to probe for what is not known) and to gain a range of insight on specific lived experiences.

In this study, semi-structured interviews began with general questions with each of the eight participants. To begin the dialogue, relevant topics such as place of birth and family background were initially identified to establish the relationship between these topics and such issues as why the individual and/or his/her family chose to move to the United States. Not all questions were designed and phrased ahead of time. The majority of questions were created during the interview, allowing both the interviewer and the person being interviewed the flexibility to probe for details or discuss issues.

The second phase used an autobiographical approach to allow the participants to write autobiographies, while providing each participant with free rein of their narrative on their lived unauthorized experiences. Lincoln and Denzin (1994) write on the benefits of such an activity by stating that it is important that the qualitative researcher study the world always from the perspective of the interacting individual.

The autobiographies were developed by asking the participants to provide the researcher with the opportunity to reflect on their own childhood and adolescence, and perhaps to come to a new or clearer understanding of the important event in their life that brought them to the United States. In writing their narratives, they were encouraged to bring their own personal experience into dialogue with the topic of negotiated lived space.

They were asked to write about significant events in their lives—"a time when something memorable happened, something powerful, something that changed you, something that helped you to understand who you are, something that you have not forgotten." They were asked to tell about their experiences, in a narrative or story form, writing in the first person, while capturing as many details and dimensions of their experience as possible. They were encouraged to be creative in their style of presentation—"You should write your account in a way that feels most comfortable and meaningful for you, in your own voice."

Case study methods were used to provide an in-depth examination of individual lived experiences as unauthorized youth/college students. According to Lamnek (2005), case study is a research approach situated between concrete data taking techniques and methodological paradigms. A case study also provides a systematic way of looking at events, collecting data, analyzing information, and reporting the results. As a result the researcher sought out to gain an understanding of why unauthorized youth/ college students find themselves in conflict and/or trauma, and what might be important to look at more extensively in future research.

Lastly, to identify the themes of issues derived from the eight collective narratives and case studies, thematic content analysis was used. In this thematic content analysis process, all data that relate to specific topics were classified as patterns using coding techniques. This was done by reviewing the researcher's notes, autobiographies and case studies as well as identifying issues that fit under a specific pattern. All identified issues were placed with a corresponding pattern. For example, when a participant named their sense of "not belonging" while they were speaking, the idea was placed under the descriptor of belongingness.

The next step of the thematic content analysis was to combine and catalogue related patterns into sub-themes. Themes are defined as units derived from patterns such as conversation topics, recurring activities, or feelings. Themes were identified by clustering together parts of ideas or experiences that were unlinked when viewed alone. Themes that emerge from the participants' stories were pieced together to form a holistic profile of their collective experiences.

Leininger (1992) states that the "coherence of ideas rests with the analyst who has rigorously studied how different ideas or components fit together in a meaningful way when linked together" (p. 60). In thematic content analysis, Ely (1989) recommends that, when gathering sub-themes to obtain a holistic view of the information, it should be easy to see a pattern emerging. When patterns emerge, it is best to obtain feedback from the participants about them.

This was done in a face-to-face interview, the last step of the interaction with the eight participants, in order for them to give feedback on their transcribed conversations (semi-structured interviews).

The last step of thematic content analysis was to build a rationale for choosing the themes. This was done by reflecting back to the research literature and the information that was obtained from the interview sessions and autobiographies. Once the themes were collected and the literature studied, the researcher formulated theme statements as part of his findings to this study.

In this study, the semi-structured interviews, autobiographies, and face-to-face dialogue were used to triangulate the data to establish meaning (Yin, 1984). An example of the process is found in Appendix E. The eight cases yielded a multi-perspective analysis by considering not just the voice and perspective of the participants, but also the relevant situations that have impacted their lives. This one aspect is a salient point in the characteristic that case studies possess. They give a voice to the powerless and voiceless.

Participant Profiles

Table 3.2 and Table 3.3 provide an overview of the background of the selected eight participants included in the study, four males and four females, of Mexican ancestry, and all four attending a college or university in Southern California. In addition, four attended a community college and four a four-year university.

GENDER	COMMUNITY COLLEGE 1 OR 2 YEARS IN COLLEGE	UNIVERSITY CSU/UC 3 + YEARS IN COLLEGE
Female	2	2
Male	2	2

Table 3.2 Participants by Gender and College Attendance

PARTICIPANT	GENDER	AGE	PLACE OF BIRTH	AGE ENTERED THE UNITED STATES UNAUTHORIZED	YEARS IN COLLEGE	MAJOR/ MINOR
1. Maria	Female	19	Michoacán, Mexico	2	Sophomore	Sociology/ English
2. Roque	Male	20	Yucatan, Mexico	3	Junior	International business
3. Linda	Female	27	Colima, Mexico	5	Graduate	Anthropology
4. Diego	Male	24	Jalisco, Mexico	11	Junior	International business
5. Norma	Female	24	Guanajuato, Mexico	4	Senior	Social Science
6. Chuy	Male	19	Guanajuato, Mexico	5	Sophomore	International business
7. Brenda	Female	20	Jalisco, Mexico	1	Freshman	Undeclared
8. Pedro	Male	19	Michoacán, Mexico	9	Sophomore	Nutrition

Table 3.3 Participants by Characteristics

Participant Profile

Maria is a nineteen-year-old female student attending a Southern California state university. She is a sophomore majoring in sociology, with a minor in English. Maria was born in Michoacán, Mexico. She entered the United States unauthorized at the age of two. She is bright, charismatic, and engaging. For most of her life she felt unaffected by her legal status until she entered college.

Roque is a twenty-one-year-old male student attending a Southern California university. He is a junior majoring in international business. Roque was born in Yucatan, Mexico. He entered the United States unauthorized at the age of three. Roque feels trapped. He is unable to share with most people his legal status, including his academic advisors. He is concerned with the requirements of his major to study one semester abroad.

Linda is a twenty-seven-year-old female student attending a Southern California state university. She is a graduate student majoring in applied anthropology. Linda was born in Colima, Mexico. She entered the United States unauthorized at the age of five. Linda is optimistic and resilient. She sees herself as a college professor. She is confident laws will change so that she can obtain permanent resident legal status in the United States.

Diego is a twenty-year-old male student attending a Southern California state university. He is a junior majoring in international business. Diego was born in Jalisco, Mexico. He entered the United States unauthorized at the age of eleven. He feels incarcerated. He has one more year to finish his degree, but future employment seems unrealistic given his legal status.

Norma is a twenty-four-year-old female student attending a Southern California state university. She is an undergraduate student majoring in social science. Norma was born in Guanajuato, Mexico. She entered the United States unauthorized at the age of four. When she contacted the researcher, the INS had recently detained her mother. She wants to obtain a teaching credential but fears her status will hinder her objectives.

Chuy is a nineteen-year-old male student attending a Southern California state university. He is a sophomore majoring in international business. Chuy was born in Queretaro, Mexico. He entered the United States unauthorized at the age of five. Diego experienced apprehension and deportation as a child. Those memories are vivid in his mind.

Brenda is a twenty-year-old female attending a Southern California community college. She is a freshman with an undeclared major. Brenda was born in Nayarit, Mexico. She entered the country unauthorized at the age of one. Immigration attorneys have extorted Brenda and her family with false promises of legal resident status, like so many others in their situation.

Pedro is a nineteen-year-old male attending a southern California community college. He is a sophomore majoring in nutrition. Pedro was born in Guerrero, Mexico. He entered the country unauthorized at the age of nine. He feels trapped and futureless where career options are concerned.

Data Collection Approach

The approach taken to collect data on the eight participants involved semi-structured interviews, autobiographical data, and face-to-face interviews.

Semi-structured interview

The following questions were used to acquire information of the negotiation of lived space on each of the eight participants. With consent permission the interviews were recorded and transcribed, all the while using their pseudonym. Before asking a series of questions, the researcher introduced himself, explained the purpose of the study, and asked if the participants has any question before asking the participants questions on their lived experiences. The respective general questions asked included:

1. Where is your family from?
2. At what age did you come to the United States?
3. What do you know as to why your family and/or parents moved to the U.S.?
4. When did you first become aware of your legal status?
5. How has your legal status affect you as a child? In your youth (teenage years)? In you present stage of your life as a college student?
6. Can you recall any positive or negative experiences in elementary school? In middle school? In high school? In college?
7. Specifically, how did your legal status affect you in the different stages of your education?
8. Given your daily-lived situations and experiences, what are the comfort zones of your daily-lived situations? What are the uncomfortable confrontation zones of your daily-lived situations?
9. Did the status of being undocumented affect your sense of identity (how you identify yourself) as a child? In your teenage years? As a college student?
10. What are the types of daily-lived situations that you confront with as undocumented youth? In your younger years, what was your sense of belonging?

11. What are the types of concerns that impact you directly as an undocumented youth negotiating your daily-lived situations?
12. How did you as an undocumented youth respond to the daily concerns and stress that you experienced on a daily basis?
13. In general, what makes you keep going in life? What are your aspirations? Do you think you are resilient (willing to forge ahead)?
14. Any other thought you wish to add, expand, or clarify on the challenges facing college-aged youth?

Autobiography

The following directions were given in the development of an autobiography:
Please use the following questions to guide the writing of an autobiography centering on your challenges in negotiating your legal status and lived space—your interactions on a daily basis.

1. Reflect on your childhood, and discuss important events that come to mind about living in the United States.
2. Reflect on your teen-age years (middle and high school years) and discuss important events that come to mind about living in the United States.
3. Reflect on your college years and discuss important events that come to mind about living in the United States.
4. You are encouraged to discuss any personal experiences and how you have negotiated lived space.
5. What have been the most significant events in your life—a time when something memorable happened, something powerful, something that changed you, something that helped you to understand who you are, and something that you have not forgotten?
6. Capture as many details and dimensions of your experiences that feels most comfortable and meaningful for you—"in your own voice."

The autobiography narratives were developed by the participants and read by the researcher. The researcher met with each of the eight participants to review vague statements and/or clarify statements about their story and lived experiences. They were asked to clarify, edit, delete, or expand on their respective narratives. The eight narratives were then analyzed for salient themes, issues, and concerns based on experiences that have impacted undocumented youth in their daily-lived situations. The follow-up on the autobiographies was a series of face-to-face meetings to follow-up on narratives to further ascertain their lived situations profile.

Data Analysis

Data analysis allowed the researcher to identify consistent themes using content analysis techniques from all the information collected, including interviews, autobiographies, and follow-up meetings. The themes of negotiated lived situations were derived using the following modified process adapted from Cortese (2003):

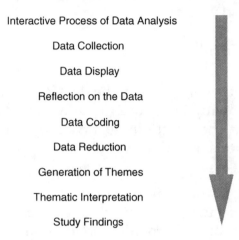

Interactive Process of Data Analysis

Data Collection

Data Display

Reflection on the Data

Data Coding

Data Reduction

Generation of Themes

Thematic Interpretation

Study Findings

Figure 3.2 Interactive Process of Data Analysis

Development of Study

The case studies and findings of the study are provided in the next three chapters. Chapter four is an autobiographical piece by the researcher, establishing the context of being undocumented through a personal reflection.

Chapter five has four sections. Part 1 consists of two case studies of two females with less than three years of college. Part 2 consists of two case studies of two males with less than three years of college. Part 3 consists of two case studies of two females with more than three years of college. Part 4 consists of two case studies of two males with more than three years of college.

Chapter six provides a discussion of the research findings that responds to the research question of the study. The chapter presents the themes that emerged from the narratives and voices of the eight participants.

Chapter seven provides a reflection of the study from the researcher's perspective and recommendations for further research. In this chapter the researcher discusses the legal, sociological, and psychological implications of the findings of this study that seek to document explicit and implicit lived spaces of unauthorized Latino youth living in the United States.

Chapter 4

Establishing the Context of the Undocumented Experience: A Personal Reflection

Out of my many childhood memories, one stands out. I vividly recall the raids by the United States Border Patrol on the migrant camp where we lived. People were screaming and running in all directions trying to avoid capture. Men were thrown to the ground and kicked by immigration officers for running away; my mother cried as her nephew, who could not escape the officers, was being taken. Of those who did not appear after the raid, people would simply say "se lo llevaron." No one doubted they would return, but we were also all aware of the looming perils.

It all seems so surreal now. The anxiety and hatred I felt then I still feel. I am certain that the things I saw and lived as a child have marked my life forever. I saw and experienced too much injustice, poverty, and death at a young age. Undoubtedly it shaped the way I see the world. It has absolutely influenced my academic work, including the subject of this study.

I find it difficult to divorce myself from something so personal. In a poem dedicated to my mother who passed away four years ago, my colleague and friend Dr. Mario Martin Flores and I captured the thoughts and memories of my childhood.

To my Mother: Wandering Homeland

For Helena Gonzalez de Jacobo

To suffer while doing good.
The pesticide cancer
To suffer
withers the flower of the lungs
while doing good.

Light reaches them through the air, death reaches them through the air,
they fall as insects into the unmarked
wounds of a foreign land,
cultivated among the pincers of a personal cancer
breathed in a thousand times.
Migrant mother, I am joined to you by the mud on your workman's boots
with that mire I made myself into a
man and unmade myself
into a son, a neighbor, a friend and a father.

Now that the toil is finished, let me
remove your shoes as when I was a child.
Remove, here, today,
the pain and weariness of the day.
The setting sun still illuminates the foreheads of the hills
and of your sons,
I want to take sanctuary in your scorched bay,
our lives are the rivers that flow into Oceanside,

which is, as all seas are, an endless dream.
Let me walk around, when you are not there,
with a familiar air
and the scarce breath of your lungs,
between the rotten winds of the planet
which have not stopped migrating
like you
always undocumented,
without fear of the final dream.

From you we emerge as earth,
to you we go with or without a laminated visa, mother.
From you the five million extinct braceros,
from your precariousness, three million invisible ones,
without laser tracks.

Trapped in the daydream of a better life,
we are all the border, there is no way to cross it,
the trick is to live in a soft voice
and die on the line.

Work inside me, mother, by the will of the Aprils of
the sowing
and the hostile harvests of time.

I reclaim you for the winters, the bites of reptile
envy and
the continental fatigue of
my deserts.

Let me adjust the stirrups
of your definitive emigration
mount the steed of peace without rest.
The work is complete
it is simply a matter of flowering
in the furrowed hand of the Sower.
There is no hurry, nor schedules,
only the time of your time,
on which everything that we are
depends.

Mi Madre: Patria Errante

Para Helena González de Jacobo

Padecer haciendo el bien.
El cáncer pesticida

Padecer

marchita la flor de los pulmones,
haciendo el bien.
Por el aire les llega la luz, por el aire la muerte,
como insectos caen entre las heridas
sin señas de una tierra ajena,
cultivada entre las tenazas mil veces respiradas
de un cáncer personal.

Me une a ti madre migrante el barro de tus botas labriegas
con ese lodo me fui haciendo
hombre y deshaciendo
en hijo, vecino, amigo y padre.
Déjame ahora que terminada la faena,
te descalce como en mi infancia.
Descalzarte hoy, aquí,
de las fatigas y dolencias de la jornada.
Aunque el sol decline, alumbra la frente de los cerros
y de tus hijos,
quiero refugiarme en tu bahía asolada,

nuestras vidas son los ríos que van a dar a Oceanside,
que es el soñar sin término, como todos los mares.

Permíteme, cuando no estés, andar por ahí,
dándome un aire de familia,
con el escaso aliento de tus pulmones,
entre el soplo podrido del planeta
que no ha dejado de migrar
como tú
siempre indocumentado,
sin azoro alguno ante el sueño final.

De ti salimos tierra,
a ti vamos con mica o sin ella, madre.
De ti los cinco millones de braceros en extinción,
de tu precariedad, tres millones de invisibles,
sin huellas láser.

Atrapados en el entresueño de mejorarnos,
la frontera somos todos, no hay forma de cruzarla,
el hecho es vivir en voz baja
y morirse en la raya.

Obra en mí, madre, según la voluntad de los abriles de siembra
y las cosechas hostiles de las eras.

Te reclamo para los inviernos, las mordidas de la envidia reptil y el agobio continental de mis
desiertos.
Déjame ajustar el estribo
a tu emigración definitiva
sube al corcel de la paz sin tregua.
La labor está cumplida
es cosa de florecer nomás
en la mano surcada del Sembrador.
No hay prisas, ni horarios,
sólo la hora de tu hora,
de la cual pende todo
lo que somos.

Although this work is not in any way intended to be a personal autobiography, it has developed into a dialectical dialogue on illegal immigration and has turned out to be very personal. I set out to conduct a study of undocumented student's views of their life utilizing micro-history and autobiographical analysis as research tools. The more I reflected on their words, however, their stories gave the impression that I was remembering old conversations of family. In many ways, their stories were my family's stories and the stories of so many thousands of other immigrants, some legal, some not. Unfortunately, these narratives have repeatedly fallen on deaf ears. An unsympathetic audience discards the voices simply as "illicit."

What took place as this work developed, were private and personal conversations that some academicians would say blur the lines of research. I beg to differ and argue that these narratives enriched our experiences, and they give true meaning to this type of investigation. They trigger awareness through humanization and conscientization of what could be a statistical worldview. Through dialogue with college-aged youth I hope to create consciousness that evokes reflection and action on the issue of undocumented youth attending American colleges.

The sociologist C. Wright Mills (1967), in his book *Sociological Imagination*, challenges a sense of civic responsibility by looking at the world through a sociological eye by noticing the connections between ourselves as individuals and patterns of society. More importantly, Mills asserts that the study of social phenomena should be the transformation of private troubles into public issue.

This study offers personal testimony of the criminalization and virtual internment of undocumented youth in the United States. This psychological, emotional, and spiritual confinement of undocumented youth is a product of historical prejudice and the failed immigration policy of the U.S. that condemns youth into a lifetime of uncertainty. While I have not experienced being undocumented, it is certainly an experience I have borne witness to. What follows is a brief look into my immigrant experience that serves to contextualize the focus of this study.

Las Raices en el Norte/The Roots in the North

According to some scholars, the Bracero Program established the contours of modern immigration flows and gave rise to the social, political, and cultural issues that dominate the discourse over immigration in the present (Jacobo, 2004).

Indeed, the importation of five million men between 1942 and 1964 into the United States as part of the Bracero Program was to have a profound socioeconomic impact both in Mexico and in the United States. It would certainly have an impact on tens of thousands of families, including my own. The lives of the poor are seldom dictated by personal choices and more so by the course set by economic and political winds in our global economy (Jacobo, 2004).

My Abuelito "Chon," short for Asuncion, came to the United States as part of the Bracero Program in 1942. He left Guanajuato with a suitcase made out of a cardboard box full of hope. My grandfather spent much of his life working north of the border looking for what in Mexico they call "una vida mejor" or a better life. My father would follow in his father's footsteps in the latter part of the Bracero Program seeking that same life.

When the Bracero Program ended in 1964, many Braceros were encouraged by their bosses to remain working with them. A large number stayed in the United States, becoming the cornerstones for Mexican American families and communities. My father did just that. His heart was in Mexico, but his common sense dictated he had to stay in the United States to improve the living condition of his family. He was soon joined by my mother who crossed the border illegally, like so many others in hopes of a better future for their families. The economic gains, however, often came at a cost. Families, children, and homes were left behind in the pursuit of a better economic livelihood.

My parents, like the majority of Mexican immigrants, did not come to the United States with the idea of staying in the United States. They were, in that sense, a prototype and stereotype of the Mexican immigrant. They came to this country with the idea of being here only for a couple of years while earning enough to build a house and buy a mule, a horse, and some cows. But two years turned to twenty and twenty turned to forty and they never went back. My mother is now buried in Oceanside, far away from where she wanted to live and die, again not by choice. Regardless of their dreams and hopes their presence in the United States gave roots to my reality and that of my children.

Mi Norte/My North

I was born in August of 1967 in Los Angeles (LA), California. My stay in LA, however, was a short one. My parents were farm workers who followed what they called "la pisca," the harvest, and were constantly on the move from northern to southern California. As such, they were unable to raise their family, and my brothers and I were sent to live with my grandparents in Acambaro, Guanajuato, Mexico. I was not even a year old when I was separated from my mother's arms. She, like the mothers of so many other children, was in "El Norte," the north, while we were in "El Sur," or the south (Mexico).

El Norte is one of those terms that one has to live, it is difficult to translate, and it is difficult to be understood. In English it is simply a cardinal point—"the north," but for us it was our livelihood, our dreams, our hope. It was everything we did not have. El Norte is, much to the misunderstanding of the larger American society, Fray Marcos de Niza's Cibola, Ponce de Leon's fountain of youth, O'Sullivan's Manifest Destiny, or the American west waiting for the plow. El *"otro lado"* is the other side of the fence (Ornelas, 2000). That is where my parents went when I was a child and where I wanted to go.

I lived the early years of my life in Guanajuato with mother's mom, my abuelita Brijida, whom we called "mama Kiki". She was a beautiful and kind old lady who for the longest time I thought was my mother. I attended school in Mexico, going first to a convent school with nuns and later to public school, *La Escuela Primaria Benito Juarez*. I have vivid memories of attending *Benito Juarez*. It was, by American standards, a school that structurally left much to be desired, but it was not too dramatically different from some of our schools in our American barrios.

The one thing I remember the most was that when I was seven years old, in my classroom there were students in their late teens also learning el *"abecedario,"* the alphabet. They had to sit in the back because they were too big and would not fit in our little desks. Mostly they came from the surrounding ranchos and were much poorer than we were. Some had no shoes and they often missed school. It was a scene straight out Mark Twain's *Huckleberry Finn* or *Tom Sawyer,* but in a twentieth-century, third-world context.

It must have been awkward and humiliating for the older students. One cannot appreciate certain things as a child, but if I could go back in time, I would applaud their strength.

I attended school in Mexico up to the second grade. In the spring of 1976, my grandmother fell ill. She could no longer care for us. We had to leave. I remember hiding in the backyard in the chicken coop, hopelessly resisting the inevitable. I held my dog, "el puma," ever so close to my chest. He did not make a sound, as if he also hoped that our silence would make us invisible. But my uncontrollable crying betrayed us, and we were caught. My time had come. At last, I too was going to El Norte.

I arrived in United States in June of 1976. It was nothing like I had seen on television. No beautiful houses with green grass to play on, only strawberry and tomato fields to work on. I remember being shocked at what I saw. In Mexico we were poor, but at least we had a house, and in California we did not even have that. We were living in the ranch where my parents worked. For years I had to sleep in a camper shell behind an old truck, often awoken by the border patrols flashlights in the middle of the night.

A few days after we arrived in San Diego from Mexico, I was taken to a school that was run by the church of my father's boss. There I was given milk and cookies and informed of my new name, "Rudy," which everyone in Mexico even now spells *Ruri*. I never had the heart to correct them, plus, for all I know maybe they are right and it is spelled *Ruri*. *Yo que se*...what I know is milk and cookies, milk and cookies; when you are a child in the United States, everything is made better with milk and cookies. This American miracle, however, does not work if you do not have a home, clothes, or, sadly, milk and cookies.

By August of that year, I started attending school at Bonsall. I remember crying when the bus picked us up. I had no idea where the hell they were taking us. I cried at school too. I had no idea where the hell I was. I cried in the classroom as well. The tears were a product of the unfamiliar cultural space. Everything was strange and, most importantly, the language. I could not understand what everyone was saying. Finally, there was a little girl, Yolanda Lopez, who came up to me and spoke to me in Spanish. Yolanda was responsible for me finding a bit of peace until at long last, I was properly situated in a bilingual education classroom. There, I knew I had found my place, kids looked like me, and they spoke like me. Those were the adaptation years. Those were good years, unlike the high school years would be.

Middle School is but a blur. All I recall is not fitting in and an array of bad grades. It was probably at this time that I realized that my family was poor. Poverty was a tremendous burden in the increasingly materialistic phase of life I was entering into. Kids can be cruel, and if you do not have the latest in fashion or gadgets, you are quickly marginalized. Often the only alternative is rebellion; if they do not want you, then they should fear you. Thus middle school years were my want-to-be-cholo (homeboy) years, marked with full social and academic rebellion.

High school memories are something most kids talk about. My brothers and I tend to ignore those years. For us they were overall difficult times. For a number of years my brothers and I were practically homeless and with incredibly limited resources. I will never forget going into the physical education building at school and exchanging clothes with other migrant children. We did this in order to avoid our schoolmates making fun of us wearing the same clothes day after day. Unfortunately those are the most powerful lessons I learned in school, the lessons about the struggles of class, social differences, prejudice, economics, race discrimination, and gender inequalities.

I also vividly remember being a part of a program called something like the Foreign Migrant Children Center. It was a center for the children of migrant workers, both legal and illegal. I have for a long time now questioned such a program. What was its purpose and what was its outcome? I recall that my first period as a senior I had Spanish class which I admit we needed since I mixed English and Spanish and was quickly forgetting my home language. I have long held the position that I never dominated either language, Spanish or English. The second, third, and fourth periods were preparing us for possible career occupations. The program, however, could have easily been accused of tracking Mexican children into the lowest paying, socially impotent careers.

I remember visiting the Bianchi leather company, the Fallbrook post office, and the United States border patrol, which my family found alarming, given the fact that half of them were in the country illegally. We never visited a professional in any other field, no engineers, medical doctors, teachers, or lawyers. It seems to me that it would have been important to show us that there were other career possibilities. We were psychologically being prepared to be the next working class underbelly of white America.

For my next class I had to sweep and mop the teacher's lounge. I got an A in that class. And for my last period I had work experience, which meant I went home and packed squash. I also received an A in that class. Not exactly college preparation courses or a core education.

How I came across college was by accident. I went on to Mesa Community College to take construction classes. My brothers and I were tired of agriculture work, and one day I decided to venture out. My odyssey took me to San Diego Mesa Community College to take wastewater technology classes. What those courses were, I still do not know. However, it was common to believe that working for the city provided good money, and I guess I thought that the class would land me a job making good money working for the city of San Diego.

One day I was looking for a vending machine when I came across the Chicano Studies bungalow. I was drawn by the posters that reminded me of myself and of Mexico. Out of the bungalow came a man who asked if he could help. He was an older gentleman with curly whitening hair. His desire to help was instrumental and forever changed my life.

His name is Cesar Gonzalez, and he was the founder of Chicano Studies at San Diego Mesa Community College and one of a number of teachers to whom I feel I owe my education. He talked me into going to college. I spent four years at Mesa College, in my opinion doing what I should have done in high school if someone, a teacher, a counselor, had taken the time to guide me. At Mesa College I started from the basics. I took basic English and basic math. And before I knew it, I was ready to transfer to a four-year university. I chose San Diego State University where I majored in United States history with a focus on international border issues.

It took me about two and a half years to finish my degree. Yet, I had never really thought of what to do with a B.A. in history. I knew I did not want to teach high school. I had been scarred by such high school memories. Luckily for me, I met another great teacher, Tom Davies, whom I credit with introducing me to graduate school. It was Tom who gave me the insight and the courage to pursue a master's degree in American History. What Cesar and Tom represent for me was the prototype of the ultimate teacher, someone who is not just a teacher in the classroom, but is involved in every space of the university, connecting with students. They, as well as others, became my inspirations to pursue a teaching career in higher education.

My Teaching

I started teaching as an adjunct lecturer at San Diego Mesa Community College some twelve years ago when I was in the last stages of my masters program in history at SDSU. My plans had been to enter a doctoral program in history, but my personal and economic reality forced me to seek a job at the conclusion of my master's degree. It was, in retrospect, a mistake. I now encourage all my students to not stop and to pursue the highest level of education available and to do so as soon as possible. Otherwise, one becomes entrenched in the system, as in my case a lecturer in higher education, and, as time passes and life takes its course it, becomes more and more difficult to complete one's goals.

2009 marked my tenth year working for San Diego State University as a lecturer in the department of Chicana/o Studies. Since the conclusion of my doctoral degree, I have obtained the position of Assistant Professor at Palomar College where I am now surrounded with AB540 Students.

Doctoral Program

There are a number of reasons why I applied to the Doctoral Program in Education. The most immediate one is the kind persistence of two professors, Rene Nunez and Alberto Ochoa. There are other reasons as well, including that I have always believed that I must continually strive to reach my full professional potential. Throughout the various stages of my life, I have always set out to be the best that I could be, whether it was working as a manual laborer in agriculture or as a student/teacher in the academic arena. This constant quest for self-improvement is a product of my mother's careful teaching: *"siempre trabaja duro y estar orgulloso de lo que haces,"* "always work hard and be proud of what you do."

My journey from the agricultural fields of San Diego County to the academic halls of San Diego State University was not an easy one. There were many obstacles which I had to overcome along the way. Over time, however, I have found that those obstacles have served to make me stronger, more focused, and much more determined. Education to me is a significant gateway to opportunity. It is the way not just to change my world but the world around us and make it what we would like it to be, a world of opportunity and justice.

My parents never received a formal education, but they knew the value of one and always instilled in us the importance of educating ourselves. I have chosen the career of teaching because I want to do my part in assuring the continual progress in our educational system in accessing equal opportunity for every low-income child. I fervently believe in social justice and in fair and equitable education for all our youth, regardless of their race, gender, religion, or economic status. This study serves as one way to document the qualitative data of undocumented space, and also to raise the social consciousness of the academy and our society in how we view, treat, and respect the human struggles of undocumented youth. The next few chapters document the voices and struggles of such college-aged youth—as they seek to negotiate their lived spaces.

Chapter 5

Case Studies of College-Aged Student Voices

This chapter presents the lived experiences of eight college-aged students using their voices and narratives.

This chapter has four sections. Part I consists of two case studies of two females with less than three years of college. Part II consists of two case studies of two males with less than three years of college. Part III consists of two case studies of two females with more than three years of college. Part IV consists of two case studies of two males with more than three years of college.

PART I

Brenda

Early Years

My name is Brenda. I was born in Guadalajara, Jalisco, Mexico. I hear it's a beautiful city, but the truth is I don't know this city at all. I only lived there the first few months of my life. Now I am twenty years old living in the beautiful city of San Diego. My parents brought me here at the age of eleven months. I don't remember this, but I heard from my parents that we crossed over through "El Cerro" or the hills. Back then they say everything was much simpler.

Elementary School

I grew up not knowing anything about my legal status and how one day it would impact me. Soon after our arrival in the United States, my little sister was born here in San Diego. Growing up, I finally had someone to play with and to fight with. It was when I would question my mom where I came from that I began to wonder. I was about seven years old at the time, and I remember feeling strange because I was from somewhere else. I didn't pay much attention to it, because when I would go play I would forget all about it. I remember when I was about ten years old, in elementary school, that some of the kids spoke English. I knew it was English that they were speaking because my mom had told me before what it sounded like. I remember asking myself if I was ever going to learn the English language, because at that time if parents wanted their children to be in Spanish speaking only classes, they were able to do so.

Middle School

It wasn't until I was going into the sixth grade that the school district decided that all the classes were going to be English only. My mom was worried because she knew now that she was not going to be able to help us with our homework. She believed that we were going to have a hard time with the schoolwork. However, it wasn't as bad as she thought; I was beginning to like it and understand it. I was having fun with my friends, because playing around and learning English was all that mattered. But time was passing us by, and we only had about three months of school left. Eventually we were going to graduate from the sixth grade and go on to junior high school.

I remember being really nervous because the teachers expected us to learn the material in English, which of course kept me thinking a lot. It was 6 A.M. and I heard a voice calling my name, "Brenda, Brenda." I woke up and saw my mom there and she told me, "Wake up, it's your first day of junior high school, and you don't want to miss your bus." Because I lived in Barrio Logan and attended a school at Point Loma (thirty minutes from home), I had to take the bus to school.

I went to school not knowing anyone; it was a different world. There were plenty of older kids who went to school with me, and that scared me. I decided to do just what I needed to do. I got my schedule and waited for the bell to ring so I could go to class. I attended all my classes and made quite a few friends throughout the year. Everything was going good. It wasn't until the next year when a lot of girls didn't like me. I didn't understand why they didn't like me, and I felt bad. Every single day I felt depressed because of these bullies. Eventually my grades suffered and I wasn't doing so well in school; I wouldn't even listen to the teachers. I was sent to the principal's office and then to a mentor because they did not know what to do with me.

Things began to change, and Tanya, my college graduate mentor, had a lot to do with it. I remember I wanted to be just like her, but I was only fourteen years old. She made life seem so easy; she had a job, a car, a good boyfriend, and schooling. I liked her life a lot. When the end of the school year approached, I had to say goodbye to her. I was left alone once more, but this time it was for good. My grades went up and I was doing well again. I finally graduated from junior high.

High School

By the time I was in high school, I knew how to speak and write in English, so I didn't have anything to worry about. It was there that the realization of inequality started. I started to see people with nice clothes, shoes, and bags. Seeing this only made me feel bad. I did not know why they had more than me. So I realized that the only way to get these things was to get a job. My mom did not have the money to pay for it because she barely had enough money to feed my sisters and me.

I was doing well in school and the bullying had stopped. I was still alone, but that was okay because I wanted to focus on school. I was sixteen years old now, and I was desperate to find a job. I went to look for one, but I soon received bad news from my mom. After I had told my mom that I wanted to work, she told me that I was not going to have luck finding a job. I couldn't get a job because I am undocumented and don't have a social security number which is required for anyone to work legally in this country.

I remember feeling really down that day because I felt as though all my dreams were thrown out the window. That same year I met a lady named Lupita. Lupita worked at a restaurant at the time, and I had told her that I wanted to work, but I didn't have papers. She looked at me and said to me, "Do you really want to work?" I jumped with excitement, and of course I said yes. She told me that she had the same problem, but she was working. She got a job at that restaurant because the owner was OK with her being illegally in the country.

I was happy to know that I could do the same. I met with the owner of the restaurant, and he said he was going pay me "under the table," which meant in cash. I felt comfortable around the staff, because they all spoke Spanish. I will never forget that day. But as time was going by I started noticing things I didn't like. I was not getting paid all the hours that I worked during the week. I worked more than forty hours a week but was getting paid for far less hours. It did not seem fair, I was getting up really early to go to school and then working so many hours and yet not paid for what I had worked.

I decided to confront the owner one day and ask him why I was not getting paid all the hours that I had worked. He replied, "You have no right to tell me what to pay you because you are an illegal immigrant, and if you don't like it I can fire you." I felt so terrible that day and I went home crying, but I did not let my mom see me or know why I was crying. Time passed by and I quit that job, but I soon got another one similar to how I got the first one. But I was getting tired of working in food service, and I wanted something more professional.

I was seventeen during my senior year and one thing I recall was that the prom was coming up soon. Prom is so costly, so I saved for a long time. It was that same year I met a teacher named Ms. Estrada, and I will never forget her. The counselors at Point Loma had accidentally placed me in her class, "Business International Trades." I felt uncomfortable because I was the only Mexican girl in the class and everyone else was white, not to mention that I didn't understand anything about business! I hated that class because everyone else seemed smarter than me, so I didn't do my work or pay attention to the lecture.

One day Ms. Estrada told me to stay after class. She told me that business was something that I should learn because in the future I was going to need it. She also boosted my confidence by telling me not to feel less, and that everyone was equal in her class. Ms. Estrada said that if I wanted to be better in life she was going to be there for me. To be honest, I needed those words of encouragement because I was beginning to give up on everything.

I began to understand business and found out that I was actually interested in it. I did so well that I ranked number one in that class and understood everything about business. There was one more thing that I had to complete before graduating and passing that class. I had to get an internship. Luckily, I found a hotel in Downtown San Diego named the Westgate Hotel. I sent my resume and a letter of recommendation from my teacher. I was really happy because I was accepted. I was also happy that I could work without a social security number because I was not getting paid.

I got a lot of experience working there in the accounting department. I realized that I liked numbers and the paperwork involved. My supervisors were very pleased with my work because I learned fast and did everything I was told. When my internship ended my supervisor called me in to speak with her. We sat down and talked about me working there as a future employee. She said that she would be thrilled if I took on the job. I was happy to hear that because I wanted to work there, but sad at the same time because I knew I couldn't. I finally told her why I couldn't work there, and she couldn't believe that I couldn't do anything about getting a social security card, or a work permit to work legally here in the country.

She began to ask me a lot of personal questions about my future and she became like a friend. I could see it in her eyes that she felt sorry for me. I went to school and told my teacher what happened and she was also surprised because she did not know that I was undocumented. All this happened about a week before I graduated, and she couldn't do much for me. I felt so angry with God that last week of high school. I wanted to do so many things, but just because I am missing a series of numbers (social security number), I couldn't even have a good job.

College

I graduated from high school and had some money saved up for college. It wasn't much different from high school, just more work in my first year at a community college. I was still searching for a way to get a social security card. Someone had told me that the easiest way to get one is to marry an American citizen. At the time I did not feel I was ready to marry anyone. One day an old friend of mine from junior high called me, and I was surprised because it had been such a long time since we last spoke. We started going out a lot and then became a couple. He knew my situation, and he wanted to do something to help me, so he asked me to marry him.

I was so confused about everything but I wanted to get my green card, so I accepted. I was already eighteen years old, and I told my mom about my plans. She was concerned but, thankfully, she stood by me and I got married. At the beginning of the marriage it was easy, but as time passed by, it got harder and harder. My husband and I argued a lot about little things. Our communication was horrible, and sometimes we would not talk for days. He expected me to feed him, but I did not know how to cook. I had to drop out of school because I no longer had money or a job. We were always arguing about everything. I felt like I was in prison; I would just stay home and not do anything.

One day I talked to my friend Lupita, the one that got me my first job. She was working at a nightclub, and she needed a girl like me to be a waitress. I was only eighteen and I knew it was illegal for me to be handling alcohol, but I needed the money, so I took the job. I started working there sixteen hours a day, from 11 A.M. to 3 A.M. I even began to lose weight, and I felt like a zombie. I was getting paid minimum wage plus tips. The money was all right, but it was the customers that I had a problem with. It was hard dealing with drunken people all the time. They would scream and curse at us waitresses and create fights.

They wanted to get more than just a simple, "Hi, how are you doing? Can I help you?" I saw many of my co-workers get spit on and harassed by the drunken customers. I was so young and saw very wrong things that people will do to each other. But I couldn't say anything, because again I did not have the right to talk. I was undocumented, and I had to always remain self-conscious about that.

Now I am twenty years old and working at a liquor store. My husband already petitioned for me to obtain legal status, and our case is in progress. However, I am afraid because my lawyer told me that I have to leave this country in order to get my green card. But I'm scared to leave because I don't know anything about the outside (Mexico). I have heard that many of the people who go to Mexico to get their green card have been tricked and left over there with no way back.

I just wish there was an easier way of doing this, and I wish there was someone out there to help me. In conclusion, not all of us have the same luck. I always think things happen for a reason. Maybe God wants me to appreciate things better or maybe he is just giving me a hard time. Nothing comes easy in this life, and, if you really want something, you have to go get it and do your best at it. I don't regret any of this because it's no one's fault.

Maria

The Beginning

The life stories we hear are moving, touching, and a reality. I would like to share with you my background, who I am, where I came from, and who I someday hope to be. It is important for me to share my story because there are many people in my same situation—many people who suffer just as much as I have, and some who have lived harsher lives than me. My name is Maria, and I am nineteen years old. Born in 1989, I was the eleventh out of twelve children in my family. I was the last and fourth girl born into this enormous family. I was born in Michoacán, Mexico, on a small ranch. I was delivered into this world by a mid-wife, not in a hospital or with the help of any legitimate doctors. I lived in Mexico for the first two years of my life. Sadly, I do not remember any of it.

All I can recall from Mexico are the stories that I have heard from my family members. According to my older brothers and sisters, my father was a very strict and a hard working man. He was the sole provider for the family. He built an estate from scratch, being the carpenter, being the breadwinner, being the person he was, he made sure we all had clothes on our backs. We were very poor, literally living off the land. My family had its own cattle, pigs, chickens, and fruit trees that we ate from. We also had a lake, where my father would fish and bring home food. This is how my elder siblings and my parents lived for many years.

My mother had three boys before having her first girl, and another two boys before having her second girl. By the time that my mother was pregnant with me, my father was extremely happy because they were having another girl. She tells me that he had changed quite a bit over the years, being much nicer to her and the children. She claims that the reason why I'm such an optimistic person is because she had a good pregnancy with me. My father was much more helpful and much more understanding with the chores that my mother had to do.

Eight days after my second birthday, my father died. I've heard different versions as to why he was climbing a 50–100 foot tree. Some of my siblings say that he was up there cutting down the tree, and others tell me that he was trying to get some kind of animal for my mom that she was craving (she was seven months pregnant with her last child). The impact of the fall is what killed him; he was bleeding from all sorts of places. They rushed him to a hospital, but it was too late. He had passed away by the time he got to the hospital. My mother was crushed, devastated, and depressed after he died. By 1991, four of my brothers were in the United States. She had nothing to hold her back in Mexico, so she made the final decision to move to "El Norte" a few weeks after the funeral.

The Big Move

We moved to the U.S. with the help of one of my aunts. She drove down to Michoacán and drove us back across the border. Luckily, border patrol was not that strict then. They only asked her for her license and she was able to cross the border with kids and my mom. We came with my mother during the middle of April, 1991, to the city of Pasadena in California. We decided to move there because my mother's cousins were already established there. With the help of my aunts, uncle, and my older siblings, we were able to rent a house. There were twelve of us living in a three-bedroom house, including my grandma and my mom.

My youngest brother was born on April 30, 1991; he was the only one in the entire family who was born in the United States and in a hospital.

My respect is tremendous toward my mom because of all the hardships that she had to endure. Her life has been anything but easy, and she has not given up yet. Coming to a different country was a difficult transition for her, especially because of the language barrier. She always tried her best to give us what she could, but even then my childhood was not the best.

Early years

Money was always an issue growing up; we barely had enough money to make ends meet. My older brothers were working two jobs, and my oldest sister had a full-time job, and she was going to high school. My mother was trying her best to make money any way she could. Because my youngest brother was born here, she was able to get assistance from the government. She was eligible for WIC (Women, Infants, and Children program) which enabled her to get food stamps and monetary assistance. In addition, her cousin introduced her to a cosmetic company (Jafra) as a way to make money. She sold to all the local Latinos in the area, financing the cosmetic products and having to go back to pick up the money (most of the time in payments).

I began going to school when I was three years old, to a Head Start program that was similar to a daycare but was also a school. My mother tells me that I loved school since I was a little girl. I quickly learned English, and also learned to read and write in both Spanish and English. I began going to prekindergarten when I was four and I stayed there all day, even though we were required to be there only for half days. I was pretty shy in elementary school. I remember my teachers were always welcoming toward me because of my older siblings. They would say, "Oh you're a (*my last name*), I had your sister or brother in my class!" I would usually get good comments from the teachers, and even the assistant principal took a special liking for my family.

The assistant principal knew almost all my brothers and sisters, and he always looked out for me. School was something I enjoyed. I liked learning about new things and getting praised for being an excellent student. Sometimes the kids were mean to me because I looked older, and I was taller than most of them. I didn't have a problem making friends, but I usually stuck to one of two girls, never really forming cliques. I never felt different from the other children I grew up with; I was never ostracized because of where I was born. If anything, the only reason I intimidated the other children was because of my height. I think the area had a lot to do with the way I looked at my status. Pasadena was not known for immigration raids, so it was something that I didn't really worry about. I was not in danger of being deported if I went to the store or on a fieldtrip; I can honestly say I felt safe going to school.

Elementary years seem like a blur to me, the only big thing that happened is my family moved from the house, to a two-bedroom apartment. We were in a tiny place for too many of us in the apartment, but it was the only thing we could afford. I remember going with my mom to sell her cosmetics all around Pasadena and dreading the walk. She would take my younger brother and me along with her because she didn't want us to be home alone. Most of my other brothers and sisters were older and able to take care of themselves, so she didn't really have to worry about them.

I was always my mom's personal translator; if she ever needed someone, I was the first to be volunteered. I remember distinctly having to go with her to the welfare offices and tell the social workers what she needed, and how our family was doing. I learned quickly that our family was not well off. Unlike most children nowadays, I was forced to grow up quickly, to mature faster than the other kids I grew up with. I knew the value of money, and what it meant to be poor. I never asked for things growing up because I knew we couldn't afford it. My clothes were mainly hand-me-downs from my sisters, and sometimes my brothers' clothes. I was lucky if I got a new pair of shoes a year. My mom would always stress about having to pay the next month's rent and/or bills. Somehow, someway, we always had food on our plate. I can honestly say that my mom made sure we had a hot meal every time we came home from school. (And her food is delicious!).

When I was ten years old, I remember meeting Guy at a Christmas tree lot close to where I lived. My brother had bothered Guy persistently for a job, working as a tip boy tying down Christmas trees on the roof of cars. He finally agreed to allow him work there and soon after, the rest of the family got to know him, as my brother's patron. He also took a special liking to me and my younger brother. We used to come around the lot just to see my brother work, and occasionally we would run errands for Guy, like getting him a soda or some food across the street.

After this Christmas season, Guy began coming around more often. He became almost like a father to me, buying me things, taking us places, and just being there. We all grew really attached to him and him to us. The following February, we were being evicted from our apartment. We had to find a place to live, quickly. Luckily, Guy helped us find a house in 1999, right before I went to middle school.

The New House

Guy was the one who did the searching for our place to live because I knew he cared about us. He looked for a place nearby where we were already living because we walked everywhere, considering that we didn't have a car. We moved in to a five-bedroom house with 1.5 bathrooms. It was such a huge transition, coming from that little apartment. Guy helped us move into that house, and he also began to live with us. I shared a room with my mom and my sister.

The house had ample room, and my mom was so much happier there. The rent of course was more expensive, but by then some of my other brothers had begun to work. The neighborhood was better than where the apartments were; we lived on a main street. That fall I entered middle school where my sister was already going. For the first time in my life, I realized that I wanted to go to college. I not only wanted to excel in school, but I wanted to pursue further education after high school.

My first progress report card from middle school showed proof that I was a talented individual. I was in the sixth grade, and I remember feeling so good about myself. Guy had promised me a large sum of money if I continued to get straight A's in my classes. I was willing to work hard and get those grades, which in the end I was able to accomplish. Guy never did give me the large sum of money, but he made me realize that I was capable of doing something with my education. My family has always looked at me as the shining star, the one who was going to do something more than just a minimum-wage-paying job.

Middle School

During my preteens I began working for Guy too at the Christmas tree lot, cashiering for him here and there, whenever I had a chance. I learned the value of money and what it meant to have your own allowance. I grew up with more responsibilities than your average teenager. In school, I was placed in advanced classes. They were more challenging and demanding than the regular or honors classes. I was doing extremely well, still receiving the majority of A's in my classes. However, I felt like I wasn't doing enough. My family has always been very proud of me, but I really felt their sense of pride throughout these years. My mom attended the open houses and back-to-school nights and spoke with all my teachers. Each time, she would hear the same thing, "Your daughter is very intelligent and motivated; she is a natural leader." Of course I still had to translate most of the time, but my mom understood with the body language from my teachers.

One of my teachers in particular, Ms. Anderson, was one of the first teachers to get me started in the path toward college. She asked me if I wanted to join Upward Bound, a college bound program that begins in the summer of eighth grade going into ninth grade. I told her that, of course, I was interested, but I wasn't sure if I could do it. Because Upward Bound is a government-funded program, they only accept U.S. citizens. I had to let her know my situation and why I wasn't born here. She then proceeded to ask me questions about my stay here and how I came here. I explained everything to her, from my father's death to my mom's personal hardships. It was not easy to tell her that I was not born here.

Although I did feel comfortable talking to her about it, it was something I felt embarrassed about. I didn't want her to pity me because I was different; I wanted her to see me for who I was. This woman will always hold a dear place in my heart because she was always there for me. Ms. Anderson talked to the director of the program and explained to her my situation. The director of the program was very understanding, and she accepted me. I was going to summer school through Upward Bound that year. That summer transformed me; I became a different person with a different agenda.

My school was grades six to twelve and I went there from beginning to end. But before the summer of eighth grade going into ninth, I decided to run for class office. I wanted to start off with something small, like secretary or treasurer, and I mentioned it to Ms. Anderson. She took the application form from me and told me that I was only going to run for president. At first, I was shocked, but then I realized that I could do it, and I could do a good job at it. I accepted her challenge and ran for ninth-grade class president. I actually campaigned by giving out stickers, making fliers, and posters. I also had to give a speech in front of my entire middle school, which consisted of at least eight hundred students. It was quite the experience! I had Ms. Anderson by my side, and she helped me with writing and proofreading my speech, in addition to offering to be my class advisor. She was one of the many people who had a positive impact on my life. Eventually, I won the election.

The summer before going to high school was very fun, and full of work. I was taking classes to get ahead in my high school curriculum through Upward Bound at Cal State LA. I was getting up at 5:45 A.M. Monday through Friday just so I could be on the bus by 6:20 to go to school twenty miles away. The program provided us with breakfast and lunch, which helped me because I didn't have to worry about eating at home. It was a very intensive program; we were in class most of the day, and right after we had mandatory tutoring hours where we could get our homework done. I made many new friends through Upward Bound, and I had a college experience even before going to high school. Throughout the years in high school, they took us to different college campuses to encourage us to go to a four-year university.

High School

As I began my freshman year, I was excited about the new opportunities available to us. I was excited about the clubs and sports we could join. I tried out for the basketball team and made varsity, but with the combined stress of my classes, being president, and working with my family, I had to quit. I created a few fundraisers for my class, trying to work my way up with more success. My classes went well; I aced almost all of them. Upward Bound had a spring break retreat incentive for their students receiving a 3.0 GPA or higher, and I was qualified to attend.

This particular year we were visiting schools south of the Los Angeles area, in San Diego. We went to University of San Diego, San Diego State University, and University of California San Diego. Out of the three schools, I liked S.D.S.U. the best because of the atmosphere and its invisible magnet. U.S.D. seemed too strict and the life of the school seemed dead. U.C.S.D. did not seem diverse enough for me; there were mainly Asians that went there, and I thought I would get lost there because the campus is so large. Right after spring break is when softball season kicked in and I began to play. I was on the junior varsity team, and I had a lot of fun playing that season. Although we weren't very good, it added to my list of things to do. I was in school from 7 A.M. to 6 P.M. throughout those days.

The following summer (before going into tenth grade) I took classes through Upward Bound again, and had an even better summer. I was recognized by my peers and my teachers as a very intelligent individual. I knew I had to be more than just your average student to go to college, so that's why I pushed myself to the limit. I was always doing something school related, or with extra-curricular activities that would show how well-rounded I was. Once again, I got top grades in my summer classes, and I started off my sophomore year on a good foot.

This is the year I discovered my love for volleyball! I tried out for the team and made it. I was nicknamed the "bullet" because of my strong arm. When we were going over serving, I hit the ball so hard it hit the other side of the wall. My height gave me an advantage with sports, and volleyball in particular. I was the middle blocker and hitter. Athletically, I was on top of my game, and I was also a natural leader. The girls would go to me for advice, even though I wasn't captain! After volleyball season came Christmas, which is when I would work with my family.

I was only sixteen years old, but I was seen as an adult in their eyes. I helped my brother with his Christmas tree lot, and I was also going to school all day. It was tough, but it was something I did every year and continued to do so until now. Coming back from winter break, I finished the school year strong (except for a low grade in my pre-calculus class). Everything seemed to be going good for me; I was doing great in school, putting on multiple fundraisers for my class, playing two sports a year (at least), and even helping my family financially.

I decided to get a job working at a clothing store right before school ended. It was a small establishment, so I was not at risk for being asked for a background check. I gave them a fake social security card that one of my brothers had asked someone to make for me, and I also gave them my school I.D. as a form of identification. I told them that I did not have a driver's license and I had not taken the time to get a California I.D. Luckily, they did not pester me about getting them the California I.D. The reason I needed a job was because I needed some form of income to pay for my expenses, because I knew I couldn't ask my mom for it. The summer before going into my junior year, I did a different program. I got connected through the director of Upward Bound to do a program that was designed to get Latinos interested in health careers. The program was called H.C.O.P. (Health Careers Opportunity program).

We took classes (for no credit), that was suppose to enrich our understanding of the sciences and of health careers. We lived at the dorms at Cal State LA for about two months. We also had a stipend to cover our food and any other expenses that we had. I lived on my own for the first time that summer, and I did just fine. I learned how to manage my time accordingly because there were no adults around. I still kept my job working at the clothing store and only worked there on weekends. Like always, I was doing a lot! I was doing this program, working, and practicing for volleyball.

By the time I got into my junior year in high school, everything was becoming routine: from fundraising money to staying at school for long hours. This year practically flew by. Before I knew it, it was summer time, and I was looking at places to have our prom. Senior year was the most memorable and stressful because this is where all my hard work had paid off. I was putting on events for the senior class, from having breakfast at the Hard Rock Café at Universal Studios to our prom at Newport Beach, I was pretty busy.

When November came around, I knew this was going to be crunch time. I had to apply for colleges, write a personal statement, etc. Once again, the problem was money. I had to pay for my applications to the schools that I could potentially attend, but I had no money. Ms. Anderson, my life savior, came to the rescue once again. She helped me fill out the forms online, and she also paid for my applications. I limited myself as far as the choices for college because of the financial burden. I still had no idea how I was going to be paying for tuition or my living expenses if I decided to move away.

So I applied to four schools: San Diego State (being my number one choice), Cal State LA (second choice only because I could commute), Cal State San Marcos, and San Jose State (I have family up north). I knew I was going to get into all those schools because I had done above and beyond in high school, but the problem was going to be paying for it. Even with the law A.B. 540, which granted me in-state tuition, I still had to pay for it out of my pocket. My family could not afford to give me close to $4,000 a year to go to school, it would be impossible.

During the month of December, a CS University employee by the name of Roberta and her colleagues recruited students from the LA area to attend a CS University through a Presidential Grant Scholarship. Thankfully, Ms. Anderson knew about this scholarship and she told me to apply for it. I talked to Roberta before actually filling it out because I wanted to make sure that I was eligible (considering my citizenship status). I gave her a little background on my life and who I was. Explaining to someone you just met your life's story within a couple minutes is never an easy thing to do, but in order to get where I wanted to be, I had no choice.

Once I told her my citizenship status, it made me feel a bit vulnerable because it was in her power to do what she could with my education. Thankfully, Roberta spoke with the director of the program and gave me the green light to go ahead and apply. With that said, I wrote down all the achievements I had completed throughout high school, and I also wrote how my mom's extraordinary life had affected me. We were supposed to find out during April or May if we got the scholarship. I was so nervous during this time, because I knew this scholarship could make or break my opportunities to go to a CS University. I got the phone call while I was working, and, thankfully, the news was good. An employee from the CS University called to tell me that I had received the maximum amount for the scholarship ($10,000). I was so excited and happy that I wanted to leave work just to tell my mom I was going to be moving away in a couple months.

When I told my mom that I had received the money to go to school and I was going to move away, she wasn't as happy as I expected her to be. I told her that I was going to be living in San Diego. She was scared for me because I was so close to the border. In addition, she also had a problem letting go of the baby of the family because she knew I was independent from her. Deep down inside she knew that I was going to be just fine living on my own, but she wanted to hold on to me for as long as she could. Eventually, that backfired on her because I moved out earlier than expected.

My mom and I were clashing about anything and everything. I took the first chance to leave with Carly, my old volleyball coach. She is a great role model and like an older sister to me. She was living in the city of Orange, in Orange County, at the time, so I was commuting back and forth to Pasadena to work. I was driving at the time, although illegally, and making that drive two or three times a week was risking a lot in itself. I would always be cautious about where I drove and how I drove. And unfortunately, the relationship that I had with my mom was not good. She didn't take my threat seriously about moving out early, but when I followed through with my word, we didn't speak for about a month. This was a really tough time for me because this is when I needed my family's support the most but had it the least. I was ostracized from the family because I was not talking to my mom, and I was also the youngest to ever move out from the house.

College

The end of August came quickly and my time was up. Carly moved me into the dorms late August and made sure that I had everything that I needed, from bed sheets to snacks in my fridge. Looking back now, I felt so lonely because none of my family knew anything about where I was living or where exactly I was going to school. I stayed in San Diego for the first month and half, resisting any urges to go back home. Although I was working during the summer, I was low on cash and I was barely making ends meet.

During the month of September I looked for ways to get involved on campus, since I was already involved in high school. I looked into M.E.C.h.A. and went to a few of their meetings. I met some interesting people through this young group of activists, but I didn't feel like I was really meant to be there. They were too extreme for my liking and I felt like they wanted to bring Mexico back to the United States.

It was a bit of a culture shock coming to school in San Diego. The majority of the people in my classes were white and I was one of the few minority students that made it to a university. Thus, I was looking for some type of support group for minority students. During the month of October I met a group of very motivated and driven women who were a part of a national sorority. I was very comfortable around them because they were like me. After much consideration and thinking, I decided that joining this sorority would be a good thing for me. With hard work and dedication, I became a sister the following February. Meanwhile, the first semester of college had flown by. I did pretty well in my classes averaging above a 3.0 GPA, and I had also reconciled with my family, but most importantly my mother. We had a much more open relationship, and I was happy to come home whenever I did.

During my second semester I met up with Roberta to catch up and talk about questions that I had. I was used to working and going to school in high school so I felt that I needed to be doing something more with my time. I definitely needed the money. She told me about a professor that just had a baby, and could use some help babysitting and/or around his office. He was very cordial toward me and, of course, I fell in love with his baby boy.

His son was four months when I met him, and I still take care of him to this day. The baby is a pleasure to watch and play with! His whole family has been very supportive and caring toward me, which I greatly appreciate. Spring semester was more challenging than the fall because I actually knew what I was getting myself into, as far as the class load. Nonetheless, I still managed to do well in my classes and maintain my high GPA.

I moved back home to Pasadena during late May, and the first thing that I thought to myself was: I need a job. I needed to come up with the first month's rent for my new apartment by the first week of August. My scholarship money would eventually cover the rest of the payments, but I needed the rent money before I would get the scholarship money. I applied to numerous retail stores and got called back from quite a few. I was interested in working at Jamba Juice because I love their smoothies and their work environment seemed fun. I was told that I got the job, but I had to wait for them to start training me. I waited for about two weeks, and I never got the call back. I kept calling and insisting to speak with the manager, but my efforts were in vain. Instead, I decided to go through with working at a retail store. I knew this job was going to be much more hectic and chaotic, but I really needed the money.

The day of our orientation they asked for two forms of identification. Luckily, I had already warned by brother that I was going to need a fake ID that verified I was a U.S. citizen. I really felt bad giving them fake, or illegal, documentation of who I was, but I had no choice. There was no way I could ask my mom for $400 just because I needed money for rent, I needed to work for what I needed. Thankfully, they did not do a background check, and I was good to go. I worked there for about two and half months and received enough hours to be able to pay for the first month's rent and also to have a little extra cash.

During this summer my sister also took me to get an ID from the Mexican consulate so I could finally open a bank account and be able to store my money. With a bank account, I also signed up for direct deposit through the school which also facilitated things for me. August was already here, and I was moving back to San Diego. This time however, Guy, my mom, and my brother moved me in. I am currently living with roommates close to campus. I was happy that my mom finally got to see San Diego for herself and also to see where I'm living. I was not able to put my name on the lease for the apartment because they asked for a social security number, which of course I don't have. Not only that, nothing is in my name (as far as bills go) because I don't have a credit history, and I am also afraid that they will ask for my social security number.

So I pay bills directly to my roommates and give them cash so they can deposit it into their accounts. It's not the way I would like things to be, but I have no choice. Once again, I am in a vulnerable position because I cannot directly pay for things nor have certain things under my name. This also has to do with trust issues as well, if I am not able to make a payment for some reason, I am screwing over my friends' credit history, not mine. I have to make sure I have the money every month to pay for rent and bills, because I am putting them at risk.

My sophomore year in college has been great so far. I took on seven classes this semester because I like to push myself, and I know I can handle it. My sorority has put on great events around the San Diego community, and I still work for the professor. Guy recently got a Christmas tree lot in the Chula Vista area, and he wanted me to help his partner run the place. Chula Vista is about twenty miles from where I live, and, considering that I don't have a car, it was going to be something difficult to agree to. I told him that I needed some type of transportation to get back and forth on a daily basis. Guy ends up renting me a car for the month of December.

Guy's partner is a recovering drug user who is trying to get back on his feet legally. His name is Clark, and he also has his nephew Allen working for him. Allen is about my age, but his maturity level is at a thirteen–year-old level. On a Tuesday night I had gotten into an argument with Clark over the way things were being done and I also indirectly told him that he needs to do something about his really lazy nephew. Allen right away got into the conversation and attacked me. I got in his face as well, but then he walked away and off the lot. Clark was worried about him and didn't care that I was upset. I come back the next day on a Wednesday night and try to make things better between Allen and I. Clark sends me to get gas down the street for the generators that are keeping the electricity going. He also tells Allen to go with me.

I don't argue with Clark about having Allen go with me because of our fight the previous night. As soon as I get to the gas station, I get out of the car and go pay for the gas. As I am walking back, a cop car pulls up right in front of the car I was driving. The cop asks me why there are no license plates on the car, and I tell him that the car is a rental and offer him the paper work. Hastily, he takes the papers and asks if I was the one driving. I was really nervous at this point, but I answer that it wasn't me that was driving.

The cop gets irritated with me quickly, and tells me not to lie to him because he saw me driving. He then proceeds to ask me for my driver's license, which of course I don't have. I tell him that I don't have the license on me, but then he asks for my S.S.# to look it up on the computer. I tell him that I don't have a license and now he asks me for an ID. I hand him my CS University ID hoping that he doesn't ask me any more questions. I was wrong. He proceeds to ask me what I'm doing there, why I am with Allen, why I don't have a California ID, and why is there $2,000 in cash in the trunk of the car.

The cop aggravates me with a million questions and finally after about an hour of them harassing us, he pulls me aside and asks me in a low voice what I doing driving a vehicle without a license? The cop makes sure to tell me how much I have put myself at risk. He threatens that he could call the border patrol and possibly deport me to Mexico; he also tells me that he could give me a ticket, and impound the car. This is the part where I break down, I begin to cry and basically tell him my life story: from being born in Mexico to finally having a $10,000 scholarship that covers my living expenses. The cop let me go, without a ticket, without impounding the car, and without calling border patrol.

I had a friend of mine come pick up the car, but I was in pieces. I kept crying, and I was a nervous wreck. When I came home that night, I couldn't even sleep. I was such a mess! I tried talking to my close friends about it, and of course my mom, but everything I did did not make me feel better. I had never encountered police that way; I had never been treated like a criminal. This incident was a huge wakeup call for me. Yes, I did come to this country illegally, but I was never treated like I was. For the first time in my life, I felt what it's like to be seen as different in someone else's eyes because I was not born in the United States.

I have never really thought about getting married to get my citizenship, but this incident really traumatized me. It has been something that I have been thinking about doing because I really want to be legal. I want to be able to drive a car with a license, and be insured. I have not been able to get behind the wheel again because of my fear of getting pulled over and/or getting the car impounded and/or getting a ticket. I am also stressed out about choosing a major and a career because of my current situation.

I want to be able to choose a career that I really want and not because I think I will be able to cheat the system. I want to be able to pay taxes and have a social security card. I am tired of acting like everything is OK and someday things are just going to magically fix themselves. I want to get married because I have fallen in love, and not because a friend of mine is doing me a favor. All of these are factors that play into my everyday life, and I have to deal with them regardless if I am an excellent student and a law-abiding person.

PART II

Chuy

Mexico

My life started when a young lady named Rita made a decision to raise a baby all by herself. Little did she know that the man she thought she knew would turn his back on her. I was born in Acambaro Guanajuato, Mexico. My life has been a struggle ever since I was born. Food was a treasure that was only available because my mother and grandparents worked all day long just to have two meals every day. My mother and I shared a room with two of my aunts, and their sons and daughters. This was my life as a little boy in Mexico.

Thankfully my mom made a vacation trip to San Diego, California to visit my tía Olga, and my tío Javier; they had a beautiful three-bedroom house that would make my mom consider a few new possibilities. This trip opened up her eyes, and not long after she returned back to Mexico, she decided to come back and make this my new hometown. Here I would have an opportunity to succeed in life, and fulfill my dreams.

Life in Mexico was hard, financially and physically. There would always be times where we had to skip a meal just so we could pay the electricity bill or the water bill. The only way to actually live a stable life was to have the whole family working and bringing money to the house. We had two rooms filled with about fifteen people living in it. I can still remember that my grandma would always wake up early just to make me some chocolate milk. Sometimes there was only enough for just a half a cup, and she would give it to me because she would rather starve herself just to know that I had eaten. Even though we weren't financially blessed, we were a close and happy family trying to survive in this country, which was so rich in culture and poverty as well.

My life in Mexico was great; as a little kid, I always enjoyed playing with my other cousins who lived in the same house as we did. The house wasn't big, but it was a house that kept my mother and me together. Since my father left when I was born, my mom had to take care of me along with the help of her parents, sisters, and brothers as well. Since I was young and didn't know much, I thought I was living the good life and that I was going to grow up and be a lawyer one day. I don't remember much about my life in Mexico, but from the stories my mother has told me, my life there was only good because I was a little kid and everyone would take care of me.

My mother tells me that if I would have grown up there, my life could have been so much different, and I would be a different man. I did go to school there and ended up failing first grade because my mother didn't get along with the teacher. At the end of the year when I had to take a test to go to the next grade level, the teacher flunked me because I didn't pronounced the "ll" syllable in the Spanish vocabulary correctly. I had to do two years of first grade. This is a reflection of how the school atmosphere was in Guanajuato, Mexico. We had to bring lunch to school because the government didn't pay for us to eat, so my mother would sometimes come to school during lunch and give me a torta or something. But life here in Mexico was good for me because it was the only place I really knew. Little did I know that my mom would soon make a decision while I was in the second grade, this decision would change my way of life.

The Decision

My mom made the decision that if we stayed in Mexico I was only going to end up like the rest of my uncles, either an alcoholic or drug abuser. Her decision was tough, due to the fact that she loved her family a lot. For a Hispanic individual, there is no worse feeling than leaving your loved ones behind, and my mother was no exception. I remember that when she told my grandparents she wanted to move to the U.S., they told her to leave me and then in a few years, she could come back to Guanajuato and bring me to the U.S.

This angered my mom, and she immediately raised her voice and declined the offer because she wasn't about to leave me, because she was leaving Mexico for me. Her decision was even tougher when I told her that very same night that she could leave me with my grandparents because I didn't want to leave with her. This made her rethink about taking me to America, but soon enough she told me about how much she wanted to move, so I could one day become a doctor. She told me how I could actually be whatever I wanted to be in life. She knew that in America school was free, and lunch was free, and that in America I would have a better chance to succeed than in Mexico.

She wanted me to have a better future and was willing to leave her family behind for me to live a better life. I can still remember the night we packed our stuff in the luggage that we were bringing to America. My mother's eyes were red from all the crying she went through, and sleepless nights she had just thinking if she was making the right decision. The next morning we got on the bus and headed to Mexico City, where we would take an airplane to the border city of Tijuana, Baja California, Mexico.

Crossing

Once we got out of the airplane we took a taxI to a hotel. I can't remember the name or where we would stay and wait for the call of the coyote. One of my uncles, my mom's brother used to cross people over, so he knew some people for us to contact to try the attempt to cross the border and meet up with my tío Javier. He was my mom's cousin and he offered us a place in his house. We called my uncle and he let the coyote know that we were there, and we didn't get a call back from the coyote until five days after we had called.

The Coyote told us to meet up with him at a place and to bring all our stuff because we were going to cross that night. We took our backpacks and were on our way. We met up with the coyote, and he collected the money, which was about one thousand dollars for the both of us. After that we were cleared. Now we were headed on our way to cross over the mountain, or el cerro. We started walking at night and we were always on the lookout for the migra. Sometimes we would run, and I could see my mother struggling to take a breath because she was tired of walking and running for six hours. It was around five in the morning when the sun was coming out, yet we were still seeing the same scene, which were dry grass and some little trees here and there. Not long after the sun was coming out, we were walking around and the coyote told all of us we better run because we have been spotted, and the migra was coming.

We kept running and didn't know where to hide. As we were running the coyote spotted the fence that would bring us closer to the United States and he got the people to jump it. We were in a rush, and as I was running I saw my mom falling behind. I tried to motivate her by telling her that we were almost there. As we got to the fence which was rusted color, I was going up when I saw my mom still down, so I came down and told her that we needed to hurry. She had my luggage and so she threw it to the other side of the fence so that she could get up the fence faster, but as she threw it the migra had arrived and told us not to move. There wasn't much to do after that. I lost my clothing that my mother had worked so hard to buy me, but then again I wasn't going to let her fall behind.

After we got caught, they made us go into the migra car, which fit about seven of us. I thought to myself, we were now on our way back to Mexico. The migra that caught us took us to a place where there was a bus and transported us back where to where we were going to get documented. I still remember my mom being upset that we got caught, and the money the coyote had taken which she had saved up for very long time. I was crying on the bus and I also saw more people, mostly Mexican who had also been caught. My mom told me to cheer up and told me that everything was going to be okay. I didn't know what her plan was, but I believed her and wiped my tears away and fell asleep in her lap. Not long after I had fallen asleep, they took us out of the bus and we were at their headquarters. We saw many migra officers there, and we got documented. They also took my prints and then took us to Tijuana on another bus.

After we were in Tijuana, we went back to the hotel we were staying at. The people there told us that there is always another day to try and cross to the land of dreams. Fortunately my mom still had some money in her pocket so we were allowed to stay there for the night. My mother made a call and told her brother what had happened. He sounded mad from what I could hear on the phone, and after she hung up, she told me that her brother was going to cross us and he wasn't going to charge us. We slept the night in the hotel, but I could see that my mother couldn't sleep because she was praying for us to cross the border, and be in my Uncle Javier's house.

The next day somebody knocked on the door around noon, and it was my uncle. My mother started crying because she hadn't seen him in about five years. My uncle told us to be ready to leave in about two hours. He gave us some food to eat because he knew we didn't have any money left. My mother and her brother talked about how my grandma missed him, and so on. Then it was time to leave. We now were going to try to cross for a second time, in hopes for a better ending this time. It was already dark, but my uncle told us that we had to go to a place where we would meet up with some other people that my uncle got money from. He was going to cross them as well. Then he took us all to the border. We were walking along the fence that was in place to keep us out. We walked for a long while before we stopped. My uncle was looking through the holes that these fences had, and we moved along the fence even more. He did this for a while until he told us to be totally quiet from now on.

We stopped in a place and saw him going up the fence in a very cautious way to see the other side. He went very cautiously because now the fence didn't have any holes. We stayed there for a long while, and he constantly told us to be quiet. Then all of sudden he said that all the migras that were at the other side had left, and told us to hurry up and jump the fence because they would be back soon. So he helped us jump the fence, and as soon as we did we ran about 120–150 meters. The fence was so high, I don't remember how we got up and jumped it; my uncle told us how and right after that the migra showed up.

The last person had just jumped the fence, and we were able to cross the fence successfully. As we jumped to other side we hit the pavement of the United States, we were finally there. Due to the fact that the migra saw us, we got a cab right away. It wasn't hard because the street was in front of us, and we got the cab and left right away. We first dropped off two of the individuals we were traveling with, and then we got dropped off and her brother walked us to my Uncle Javier's house. We made it, WE FINALLY WERE IN AMERICA, WHERE DREAMS COME TRUE.

Finally en el Norte: The United States

Living with my tía was a blessing and at times a bit of a pain. It was a blessing because she allowed us to stay in her house. Nights were warm even though we slept on the carpet floor that had stains already. My mother always made the best of it by telling me stories about her childhood so I could go to sleep. Due to the fact that we were guests in my tía's house, my mother offered to help out around the house in anything that she felt needed. Even with cleaning up and preparing food for the entire family, which consisted of my tía Olga, my uncle, my three cousins, and my cousin's husband, and her son.

My mom's helping eventually turned into a maid, where my mom actually had to work for the food and for the place we were staying in, which was our house. Since we were illegal, my mom couldn't get a job, and so she became the maid and was not a cousin anymore. She worked so much but every night she would put a happy and energetic face on in front of me, but I knew that behind those big eyes she was tired of being a maid but had no other option. They took advantage of my mom, and so the blessing slowly turned into a pain, watching my mom work so hard every month and she would only get $200 dollars at the end of the month.

When we started living with my tía, I was happy because I was able to interact and play with my other cousins that were about the same age as me. Coming here was hard, but my mom had a plan for me. She wanted me to go to an elementary school that was only two blocks away from where we were staying. She found the details about what she needed for me to register for school, and she got all the needed information about my schooling in Mexico, and then signed me up to go.

It started in September, so I had all summer to relax, since it was barely July of 1994. During the summer I had the opportunity to get used to this new home that wasn't our home but still was a place where we lived. I got to know my cousins and some of my tía's family, whom I had never met; they were all very welcoming to my mom and gave her hope by letting her know that she wasn't alone in this new place called San Diego, California.

After all the fun and playing during the summer, it was time to start my new school. I had no idea what to expect. I didn't know if classes were going to be in English or in Spanish, or a mix between both. I remember being excited yet afraid. My mom took me to class and told the teacher that I was the new student. She asked for my name and I told her my full name. Since this is America she asked me, by which name I wanted to be called, and I said Jesus. I couldn't have two last names, so she let me pick one of them, and I picked my grandfather's last name. So from that moment on I only carry one last name. It was a change for me because in Mexico I was called by my whole name.

The class was taught in Spanish, but we also learned English every day. I was behind from the rest of my class because the majority already knew the ABCs in English and Spanish, and they also knew the numbers. It took me a while to learn them, but before the end of the year I was getting better and better at English. I remember coming home every day from school with a smile because, unlike Mexico, lunch was free. We didn't have to pay for the food. All we had to do was fill out a paper to see if we were eligible to get free lunch based on my parent's income and, of course, I passed it with flying colors. I don't think I ever met someone who got rejected to get free lunch from the barrio I lived in.

Elementary was a happy experience in my life, being here in America as opposed to where my other cousins were in Mexico. I soon realized that this country had so many opportunities for success and the education was also free. I got to learn English, thanks to my teachers and my cousin Eddie, who at the time was in high school. Every time I came home, he would teach me some words in English and coach me on how to use the words and when to use them. Thanks to him I actually learned English faster than I would just by having the school teach me.

Elementary was good, I had good grades, many awards, and was recognized as one of the schools leaders when I had my promotion in sixth grade. All of my teachers knew me by how smart I was compared to the rest of the students. It was in elementary where I actually felt that this was my home country, I got to meet many new friends throughout school and made new bonds with the teachers as well, something that I didn't have in Mexico's schooling.

At the start of sixth grade at my elementary school, I ended up moving out from my aunt's house. My mom and I moved in with this man that she had been dating for a while; the odd thing is that we only moved to some apartments that were just two blocks away from my aunt's house. It was a big change for me, and from what I remember, my uncle and my aunt told me that if we moved that our future was going to be over. Little did I know that they were telling my mom this because they still wanted to keep her as a housemaid, and they knew that if she was gone, that they would never find someone else to do the same work for the amount they paid her.

Furthermore, during my sixth grade I had the opportunity to get my papers through an arranged fake marriage that my mother went through with a friend of my aunt's oldest son. The marriage happened about two years before we moved out, and now I was in sixth grade. I was to be interviewed or something like that, and the immigration was going to ask me some questions about the marriage and if I had answered the questions right, then I would have gotten my papers. So the guy that my mom was married to came a week before the immigration appointment. He started to quiz me and told me everything I needed to say.

So when the day came up I was ready, I got up early and we waited for him, I didn't even go to school because I was finally going to get my papers. Well, it turns out that the guy that my mom married decided to not show up because he was afraid of going to jail if they found out that it was fake marriage, just so my mother and I could both get our papers in this country. I had the chance to get my papers at a young age, but just because that guy was too scared, I am still an illegal immigrant. I was a good student during my elementary years, and now I was on my way to junior high.

From elementary school, my mother decided to put me in Correia Jr. High, as opposed to where all my friends were going; this was Memorial Jr. High. Memorial Jr. High was known to change people; the reputation that it had was that it was a gangster school where teachers really didn't care about the students because of the many fights that occurred on campus. Therefore, my mother decided to send me to Correia Jr. High which was located in Point Loma and was at the opposite side of the barrio where I lived.

Only English Spoken in Class Now

Junior High at last, now I had to take the bus to get to school. Little did I know that this would become a daily routine even after graduating from high school. It was my first time taking the bus to go to Jr. High, and there were some faces I recognized as I was waiting for the bus to come. It was good to know that I wasn't the only one that was going to go to this Jr. High.

My cousin Rita was there, too; we've practically been going to the same school ever since I can remember. When we got to campus, they took us to the auditorium where they welcomed us, and then we were sent to our classes. Now we had seven different classes that we had to attend every day. It was something new; the teachers would only speak to me in English because now the teachers did not speak Spanish, as it was in elementary.

It was a big change for me, and my English accent wasn't very good. I would get nervous every time I would talk to the teachers, I was scared for the first time, seeing a lot of white people talk English so fluently, yet there were only a couple of Mexicans attending that Jr. High. The population was a drastic change to what I was use to in elementary, and it wasn't like I had never seen white people before, but it was nerve racking that there were so many of them in this one school where the rich lived. Now I realized why my mother didn't want me to stay with my friends at the other Jr. High, Memorial, because this school was full of people who weren't in gangs and, therefore, I wouldn't turn out like one of my mom's brothers.

It was a hard adjustment to come to Correia Jr. High, knowing that I really didn't have as many friends as I used to. But it was all for the better. I remember the first classes of the semester being pretty hectic, trying to understand and write in English was hard. I spent a lot of time learning, and, before I knew it, I was actually getting better. I wasn't the only one with this problem. There were many like me, but the difference is that they didn't want to learn how to write in English because it was a change and this change was bad in their perspective.

I admit that at first I didn't want to learn how to write in English just because it was the only subject that I wasn't good at, but then I thought about it and realized that I would have to learn how to write sooner or later, and sooner was better than later. This transition was for the best; it made me realize that classes were going to be taught in English and not Spanish anymore. I adjusted pretty well, and my lunch was still free. I received good grades, even though I was a "vago" hanging with the wrong crowd at times.

This point in my life, I saw many of my friends get into drugs and alcohol. They would try to get me to join them, I never did because ever since I was little I promised my mother I wouldn't drink or do drugs. I promised her this because I witnessed what my uncles had done with drugs or alcohol abuse. My perception was set at an early age. It was this perception that I believe steered me into the right direction, where I would have a chance to make it in this country. I saw the effects drugs and alcohol had on my other friends and how they would look forward to get out of school and get high next to the park because they gave up all hope in continuing with their education and their parents allowed them to. Some of them even dropped out of school.

Junior high was tough for a while until I got used to the language, and then I realized that I could make it in this country. Adjusting to English only was a bump in the road. Once I got over it, I learned a lot more and it gave me the opportunity for me to be bilingual which opened up many opportunities. Drugs, being used and abused was a daily ritual for my friends in school and around my neighborhood.

When I met people, they never believed me that I didn't smoke weed or drink, whether they were white, Latino, Asian, you name it. It was as if they stereotyped my face as a Mexican, which meant someone who is in possession and had a great knowledge of drugs and using drugs. It was sad being stereotyped, but then again I saw that I was unique, and this uniqueness was nothing to be ashamed of. I was athletic, talented, and my physical fitness coaches always knew I would win the running events. I ran track and field for the school.

I also stayed clear of the drugs because I was on the team and I would always do well. Since I was into sports, my mind was occupied with trying to be better and faster the next time I ran. My mindset also kept me occupied and away from doing drugs. Once I was done with junior high, I was on my way to high school, but during the summer my little sister Martha was born. She was born in August, and it was about time that my mother and my stepdad had a child. It was a change that made me mature and become more responsible. It felt good not being the only child in the house anymore.

Noticing the Difference Between Legal and Illegal

It wasn't until I got to high school that I started to feel different from the rest of the student body on my campus while attending Point Loma High. Since I started to attend school in second grade, I really didn't feel left out from the rest of the students. Anything they did, I was able to do as well. This soon changed after I got into high school. At this time in my life I had some pretty good friends who knew almost everything about me, where I lived, what my favorite song was, etc. They knew everything except one thing, and that was that I was an illegal immigrant and I didn't have my papers in this country. Starting high school I was confident that I was going to play many sports, football, and others.

On the second day of school I found out that, if I wanted to join football, I had to give about $200 to be on the team. This money would go toward buying all the necessary gear and equipment I needed to play. Since my family wasn't financially stable, I couldn't really pay that amount and so I stayed away from sports for that fall season. Classes were interesting; I got into honors physics, which you have to get recommended by your previous teacher in Jr. High. Although English class was still hard for me, I hung around with the same friends from Jr. High because usually if you go to Correia you automatically get into Point Loma High. Going to high school was unusual for someone like me whose family never really graduated from high school in Mexico. It was expected of me not to make it. So going to school every day was one more day of education that no one in my family history had received.

It wasn't until I ran track and field that I realized that people were classified as an alien just because I didn't have the privilege to be born in this country. I remember being in cross country and my physical fitness coach in P.E. recommended that I be on the track and field team for the 100 meter dash, but ended up doing the one mile, two mile, half of mile, and the 400 meter relay. Being on the team was good because it got me more interested in going to school every day. It was something that I looked forward to each morning I went to school. But then our coach told us that we had to compete in Los Angeles in a meet that was pretty big; this is when I got frightened and didn't know whether or not to tell my coach that I didn't have my papers.

This wasn't my first time going to L.A. I had been there with my godmother many times, but since this time I was going with the school I didn't know if they were going to check social security numbers and so forth. So I went to one of my friends that I knew since middle school who was also on the team and told him about my residency status. He told me that it was okay because they don't really check or stop us. He said that since we are from the school, they don't mess with us, because it would look bad to the border patrol taking a student away from his team in front of his school's track and field team.

So I went to the meet because I thought it was okay. I couldn't help but to think otherwise, but, sure enough, nothing happened. It may have been because my coach had really white skin, with a mix of blonde and orange hair, and blue eyes. He was driving the van that took our team the distance to Los Angeles. I got over my fear and continued to join the cross country, soccer, and track and field teams during my school years.

My freshman year I saw how different I was because I was unable to work or drive a vehicle. It was around the end of my freshmen year when some of my friends were talking about getting cars and fixing them up once they got their license. Since I'm an illegal immigrant, I don't have the privilege of applying for a license or a job, which only made life harder for me because it prohibited me from working to earn money to buy a car or clothes that I really wanted. So I went to my mother and asked her if there was anything that I could do to get my papers, and she told me that she had tried but that there wasn't anything for me. She also told me that she soon would get married to my stepdad who was the father of my little sister Martha, and as soon as they got married I would get my papers very fast.

The only problem was that my stepdad was still married and, therefore, they were unable to get married. As soon as my friends got their cars, I started to see less and less of them because I was the only one riding the bus now. I was starting to notice the changes in my life without my papers. Instead of being upset, I would look at the situation positively by not having to waste gas to go to school. It helped keep my spirits up.

My spirits weren't high for long because not having my papers would come to haunt me again. During my freshman year some of my friends turned sixteen, and they were given the privilege to work. Since I don't have my papers, I am unable to apply for a job because I needed a social security number, something I didn't have. I realized that nothing was really going to change my residency status here in America, so I looked for other ways that I could make money. Even though I was still fifteen years old, I figured that if I could get a job right now at fifteen, then there would be no need for me to be a resident. I looked at my options and, since I have some uncles that live here, I asked them for jobs. All of my uncles either worked as gardeners, construction workers, or fixed up cars as mechanics.

Fortunately, I had these options; I asked them and they said I was too little, but if they found a job that didn't required that much muscle power, than I could work. But even then I didn't want to wait, and so I was persistent in asking my stepdad to take me to work with him when he had side jobs. After asking for about a month, he finally took me and I showed him that I was a fast and energetic worker, which made him realize that I was eager to work to get extra money, which I would use to spend on clothes or something that I really wanted.

After my freshman year I played sports again. Going to Los Angeles, Long Beach, Sacramento, Irvine, etc., would be weekend trips for me when I was in cross country and every other week when I would run track and field. I guess that playing and being busy running and being on school teams gave me the strength and the motivation that I needed to continue with school, as opposed to my friends. I had some friends who were involved in drugs and some friends who started to join gangs as a way to keep their social life going. Three of my friends that I knew almost all through school ended up joining a fake family known as gangs.

Now here is the thing, they had good mothers and their dads treated them right, so they really had no reason to join a gang. But the social life in the barrio is that, if you don't belong in a gang, you are a loner, gay, a geek, or they simply didn't like you. They joined the gangs to feel welcomed in a family, and it gave them something to do. They would also join a gang as a way to show people that their status in the barrio was higher than someone who wasn't a member of a gang. I'm saying all of this because most of the people I know who didn't have their papers ended up joining gangs. I believe it was a way to help them feel special and be a part of something that could maybe get them money by selling drugs. To sell drugs there was no need to be a resident of this country.

There are limited things that a teenager can do without having papers in this country. Thankfully one of them is going to school and getting good grades, and to hope for the best, the best meaning, going to college. Others choose alternative options and one of them is dropping out of school, and getting a job, and another one is just simple joining gangs. I decided to do none of the last two and since I was a smart kid. I knew that if I was to have a future in this country, it was going to be through my education, not through being a criminal or just working to get money right away.

I got good grades and was a good athlete as well. All of my coaches knew my name and expected me to make it big in running, but all of that changed when I had a close encounter with death. You see, in my junior year I was still running cross country for the school. Everything was going okay; we had new guys joining the team and I got to know them, one of them being Kevin. He was pretty tall, athletic, and a very fast runner. He had a bright future until one day when we went for our regular routine of running out of campus with the coach by our side. We were running and Evan was next to me, I sped up and told him to keep up so I could challenge him and urge him to go faster. I was in front of him by ten feet, when I heard about four gun shots fired in the back of me. It was a guy who was shooting at Kevin. As Kevin went down the guy kept shooting at him until he had no more bullets, and then he ran to his car and left.

I tried to get close, but my other friends pushed me to get out of the way. Once the guy left I ran toward Kevin and noticed that he wasn't going to make it. He was only fourteen years old, and the guy who shot him was his dad. His father didn't live for long, after they found out who it was, the swat team came to his house where, after ten hours of waiting to arrest him, he committed suicide. I am telling you this story because after this, I really didn't try to do my best in sports. The school did provide a psychologist free of charge, but it wasn't enough. I had given up my hope in school and on God.

My junior year in high school was not that pleasant; I kept running and was on the soccer and track and field team. I really don't know how I got good grades, I feel as if they felt sorry for what happened to me. My cross country coach and all the P.E. staff notified my teachers of the situation and why I wasn't paying much attention in school. I believe they felt sympathy for me and so they gave me A's or B's. When summer came around, I was more stable and I got back to my old self, or at least close to it. Many changes had happened, all of my friends had cars now, and so they didn't take the school bus anymore.

My friends were working as well, which gave them the money necessary to fulfill their needs to buy the latest fashion of clothes. I was still working with my stepdad and now with my uncles every now and then when they needed help. I was still telling my mom if there was anything that I could do for my papers, because I knew that if I was to go to college I would need financial help and I could only get it by being legal here. I still got the same answer, she was going to get married to my stepdad as soon as he would get divorced, and I would have my papers in a matter of two months or so.

So I stayed with the same old routine as the previous years of my high school days. I knew this was going to be the last year of high school, and so I took some Advance Placement classes to give me credit for college in case I would make it. I started to apply for universities here and there starting in October. It was kind of hard to put nothing in the social security box, every time I would fill one of them out, I didn't know if I would be let in without being a resident. I knew I would have a good chance of getting into the U.C.'s and the CS Universities that I applied to, but the absence of being here legally made me doubt myself.

I didn't do much the first half of my senior year. Since I had been running for the school for four years, one of the cross country coaches told me that there was going to be a scholarship that was titled Kevin, and he told me that if I applied I could have a good chance of getting it because he was the one in charge of picking the winner. I tried to apply for it, but since it required a social security number, I really couldn't do much. The coach would tell me if I had applied and I would say no, so he was persistent on telling me to apply. I always said I would do it tomorrow because I didn't have the guts to tell him that I was unable to get it because of my legal status in this country.

When March came around, I started to receive the letters of acceptance or rejections from the universities I applied to. I got into UCSD, UC Riverside, and UC Irvine, SDSU, SFSU, and SMSU. I was glad to see that I was accepted in all of these universities. My mom would see the envelopes that would come, and I would only tell her that they were still thinking about accepting me. I did this because I didn't want her to feel guilty that I was getting accepted and not being able to go because I didn't have my social security number.

Without a social security number, I couldn't get any financial aid or grants, so if it came down to it I would have to just get into the one that was most affordable. I looked at the prices of all the universities, and the cheapest ones that I found were CS Universities. UC's were relatively high priced, and after I did the entire math, it seemed virtually impossible to attend there, even with my parents help.

So I decided to go to a CS University. When I told my friends this, they were all surprised to see me, an individual with no papers and no help from the government still making it to college as opposed to them, who were looking forward to community college. I wanted to go to community college as well, just for the fact that I could save some money and pay a lower tuition and maybe reapply to a university. But when I told my parents this plan, they told me to go to a CS University because I was already accepted, and they would help me pay my tuition. This all took place in March of 2005, but when April came around my mom had another baby, my little sister Guadalupe, on April 2. There were some complications during the birth and they told us that she had about three holes in her heart, and that she would only live for three to five weeks.

My sister also was born with Down-Syndrome and the hospital asked us if we could give her away to the hospital where they do tests on the babies and drug them with new drugs. We immediately said no and we hoped for the best, my mom prayed and so did all the family. At this time I didn't know whether I should still be going to school because I only had two more months or go out and work to pay the bills that were piling up. After much review and talks with my mother, I kept going to school and visiting my baby sister Guadalupe with my stepdad and my other little sister Martha every day. It was then that I realized that without my papers and license I was limited to visiting my mom and sister, which seemed necessary at this time.

Going to visit my sister in the Children's Hospital was very difficult, but luckily my baby sister was strong and our prayers were answered and she stayed with us regardless of what the doctors believed. She kept getting better, but, since she couldn't eat by mouth, they ended up putting a tube to her stomach so she could get her food some way. When she was better, we took her to our house, but she kept getting sicker, so we would bring her back to the hospital. Thankfully though, when I was about to graduate from high school she was good and my whole family was able to be there, including my cousins who I had grown up with. Graduation was good, and I felt like I had made a huge achievement to myself because none of my uncles or anyone in mom's side of the family had achieved that. It gave me a little boost of motivation to continue with my education.

Money Is Scarce for an Illegal

Money was scarce, but to an illegal immigrant money was even harder to get. We don't have the right to work in this country, nor did we get any government help, to provide for people like me, who wished to keep going and continue their education. We are left out from the rest of the students who wish to go to college, and since we can't work, we have to find other means to pay for our education.

For me it was the summer after I graduated high school. Although it was fun hanging out with my friends that summer of 2005, I knew that if I wished to go to college I would have to find ways to get money, because I wasn't going to let my parents pay for it. Also my baby sister had special needs and needed extra care; I wasn't going to make my mother work just so that I could pay the tuition bills. So I asked my uncle if he could find me a stable job doing construction or any job that I could get where I wouldn't need to have my papers to get the job. He said he had nothing, but that he would have more work for me now that I needed more money; the same thing went for my stepdad.

He would give me work when there was an opportunity during the whole summer, I ended up getting about $2,500 dollars, two thousand which I saved for tuition and the rest was spent buying groceries and paying for rent at my house as well. I paid rent because, even though I lived at home, I wanted to help out by paying rent and buying groceries. So this is how I made my money for the first semester of college at a CS University.

For the second semester, I worked on the weekends, which gave me an income of about $450 dollars a month from September to December. I would save it all every month. When it came down to pay my second semesters tuition, I barely had enough to cover all the cost of books and for my trolley and bus pass for the semester.

Finally, Making It to College

My first day in college was definitely an experience that caused me much pain, but in the end it was worth it. The first day of classes were surprising;

first of all I saw many Anglo and white people, Asians, but a few Hispanic people. Although my high school was much the same way, this time there were not that many Hispanic people. This made me realize that I was one of a few Hispanics to attend this university, and I felt a boost of motivation to show the world that Hispanics are coming up in the university atmosphere. I did see about twenty familiar faces, some were friends at state, three of them were Hispanic, and I was the only illegal immigrant. Although I did see many friends from high school come here, most of my Hispanic friends had gone to community college or decided to work and make money right away. At first it was hard to get adjusted to this new system of teaching, but I ended up adapting to it.

Getting to school every day was a pain in the butt, because I no longer had free transportation. Since I didn't have a car and, even if I did, I wouldn't risk driving it because I had no license. If it came down to the worst case scenario, I would get deported and leave my mother to take care of my little sisters by herself, and I could not have that on my conscience. I decided to take the city bus; it took me anywhere from one and a half hours to two hours to get to State and the same amount to go back home.

I lived two miles down south of Chicano park, but since there's no trolley it took me longer because it is within the city. Taking the bus the first day was a shock to me, realizing how long it took me just to get to State and back home. Since it took me a long time, I decided that instead of wasting my time looking at other people just come and go from the bus I could use that time to study or work on some homework that I had. So I did, and this way I was more efficient with my time, but even after doing my homework and assignments on the bus or trolley, it was hard because I would get motion sickness here and there.

It was hard going to school every day, and I knew that I would have to be persistent if I wanted to make it through college. Although it was a pain in the butt coming and going from school, I realized that I was the only hope that my family had for success and a stable life in this country. Even though I don't have my papers, I do have a burning desire to succeed and buy my mother a house and make sure that my little sister Martha goes to college as well. My mother is about forty, my stepdad is in his mid-fifties, and my little sister Martha is seven. When I started my freshman year in college, my baby sister Guadalupe was barely a few months old. She is now three years old and Martha is now seven. So, as you can see, it's up to me to take care of the family. I am not complaining about this responsibility, but I thank God that I got to see what way to go.

In my freshman year of college, I knew that I had to keep getting up three hours before my class just so that I could have enough time to get ready for school and take the bus in order to come to college. The other part of the formula was getting serious about college, even though I had made it to a CS University, the real task began when I had to take tests and turn in homework. I could no longer mess around, so I took school seriously.

My first year in college I was not very social, but very goal oriented. I did meet a few people here and there, but since I didn't live in the dorms it was hard for me to really get close with anyone or have good friends. I would only come to school for my classes and do homework during my breaks. I would maybe eat lunch if I had enough money, and then after I was done with my classes I would go home and help out my mother around the house or do some homework, and then finally go to sleep. This was my routine for my freshman year. I did get good grades, A's and B's, and the only C's I got were from CCS 141B and CCS 100. I did achieve my goals, which were to make it on my first year with a 3.0 or higher GPA. I ended up getting a 3.35 GPA in the end. Academically I had prospered and I was proud of myself.

Being in college was a privilege, yet the social atmosphere was limited for people like me. Usually by now people are of legal age, and, since we are so close to the border, people want to go to TJ, a place to go clubbing and be able to drink legally. The friends that I made at State in my freshman year would always call my cell and tell me to go with them to TJ. I would always tell them some story like, "No, I can't, I'm babysitting," or "No, I can't, I have to go to work tomorrow at five in the morning."

They would always keep asking, so I came up with a story to tell them why I would not go back. I told them I was once in TJ when I was sixteen years old with my friends and we were just walking around just to see what things we wanted to buy, when some guys came to us and beat the living shit out of us. My friend, being a tough guy, got up and talked smack back to them until they pulled a gun and shot him in front of my face. Coming back to San Diego I told his mom, and, well, it was an experience that still haunts me. THAT'S WHY I DON'T GO TO TJ.

After I told them this little lie, they would never try to persuade me to go to TJ with them again. I know this made-up story is bad in a sense of why make up that story instead of telling them the truth. The truth is that I didn't trust them. It's hard for me to come out to someone and tell them, yeah, I am an illegal so I can't go to Mexico. Being an illegal, I have to watch my moves; I can't go around telling people or friends that I just met that I'm an alien, because, when it comes down to it, maybe one of them doesn't like me or feels that his girl in onto me, so he calls the migra on me, and my whole journey that I've made to college is done.

Second Year: Getting Harder

After my first year in college, I felt good in the fact that I was making it in this university, but now the money issue was increasing even more than before. During the summer of 2006, the summer before I became a sophomore, I had to work even harder because I had to save up money for my tuition, but further more I had to provide crucial financial assistance to my family as well. So, lucky me, my uncle needed a full-time worker in June and, since I was out of school, I worked with him for two months.

The pay was good $10 an hour for eight hours, five days a week. I gave my family money to pay the bills and on top of that I had to pay for my own tuition and still pay rent on my house. I stopped working for my uncle in the first week of August; the work with my uncle generated a fair amount of money to pay my bills. Once again I barely made enough money to continue to go to college. My parents didn't really have money, so that's why they weren't really helping me out with my tuition. I helped them and it always gave me a motivational boost every time I would buy groceries and see my little sister eat her "Lunchables."

This time when school started, I felt more confident and was taking eight classes at the time. Furthermore it was this semester when I got to be social and find other people who were going through the same thing I was, being an illegal and still coming to college. Around the fifth week of school I was approached by these fraternity guys that seemed very humble and cool, it was awesome to see other Hispanics coming together with the sole purpose of helping the community and making sure we do graduate from college, so I pledged to their fraternity.

Pledging was an experienced that helped me grow as an individual and as a man. It also provided me with the opportunity to socialize with new people, most of which were Chicanos. Being around more Mexican people made me realize that if, we stick together for a common purpose, which is to make it through college, then maybe more of us Hispanics attending college could graduate. Pledging did take a lot of my time, but it was all for a reason. We had mandatory study hours, and that made me stay in the library more often.

Pledging was a good result because, now every time I walk to my class, I see someone who I know, who is part of a fraternity. I was becoming social with all kinds of people, especially with the Chicanos. It was this feeling that made coming to school more fulfilling than before. Now when I came to school, I would stay longer talking to my friends and go to the bowling alley, and just kick it. When I was pledging, I was still working and on top of that I was taking eight classes. I was taking eight classes because my theory at the time was that if I could take these eight classes, one of them was one unit and another was two units, then I could become a junior at the end of my first semester as a sophomore. Taking eight classes would soon come back to haunt me.

Taking eight classes is almost double the amount that is required just to be a full-time student. During this first semester of my sophomore year, I still had to work and I was pledging this fraternity and helping out my family as well. It was a workload, but the fraternity was there to help me. I wouldn't pledge a fraternity if I didn't believe in it; they were the ones that were encouraging me to keep my grades up and take care of my family.

During this semester I did fall back many times on my reading, and, since I had to buy all the textbooks, I had to wait for my uncle to pay me because there were just too many texts to buy and I had little money to spend on them. Money was scarce and my budget kept getting smaller and smaller every week. Since I was on campus more now, I had to buy lunch here and there and, well, sometimes my friends who I was pledging with paid for me. One of them was an illegal immigrant as well. I won't mention names, but it was good to know that there were more of us attending college.

Since I was still working, I managed to save some money, but this time it wasn't enough. Having a lot of responsibilities this semester made me get low grades, I got below a 2.0 this semester, and unfortunately that made me get dropped from pledging because of grades. It was too much of a workload and finals killed me. There was one day where I had four finals on one day. Even though I had a good GPA, going into finals, above a 2.6, nothing could have prepared me for those seven finals I took in a week.

Now I had another problem, I had to pay my tuition, and I didn't have that much money to pay for it all. I had only saved up a portion of the amount of money I needed to pay the tuition fee I had. This is when my friends told me about the installment plan, where I could pay my whole tuition into three payments. So I paid the first payment on December, but I was beginning to fall short and be late on my payments for school. When the next semester began I was still trying to get money to buy my books and to pay my tuition. It was hard to make the money because at this time, my stepdad wasn't getting much from his work, and so I had to provide my family with financial help once again. It was this help that put me in jeopardy of not paying my tuition and made me not get my textbooks for my classes that semester. That is also the reason I did bad that semester as well.

When junior year came, it wasn't much of a difference pertaining to my financial status. I was still helping out the family and I wasn't getting my textbooks. What really helped me out was that, since I decided to pledge again for the fraternity, some of my bros had the books I needed, so this helped me out. They have also bought me lunch when I didn't have money to buy it myself. It was beginning to get harder to come to school now because since I didn't have money, I was beginning to think if I wanted to continue with my schooling I loved learning but what is the use of coming to school if I didn't have the necessary materials to succeed, like textbooks to start with.

Around this time I got my cell phone cut off because I just couldn't afford to have that luxury any more. This junior year was by far one of the worst ones, it was like my sophomore year, but the only difference was that I was beginning to think about dropping out of college. This is where my illegal status comes into play, since I couldn't work, and I couldn't get any financial help at all from any place, my education was at question just because I did not have enough money to pay the bills while I was helping out my family.

I believe this may be the case of many people like me. Where we come to this country to succeed, but then again, one has to make a decision of whether to continue with his or her education, or to watch their little sisters, and their family starve themselves and suffer financial problems, if one wants to continue school. I did both, helped out my family, and went to school. Although my grades weren't great, I was still making it.

To make my long story short, I had doubts about myself, whether or not if I could make it in college. I thought that I couldn't make it, but my desire to succeed and my desire to take care of my family is what kept me going forward and made me not give up in continuing with my education. I admit that right now, I am going through more financial problems. I am about two months overdue on my tuition, which I'm going to have to pay during the winter break because the money that I'm making right now is going to my family to pay rent, bills, etc.

I believe this year, my senior year has been the toughest because, even though I could graduate this upcoming May, I decided to double major in Pre-professional Economics, and Statistics the science of data and analysis, with a minor in Spanish, which I only need one more class to get. As you can see, I could have graduated with just a minor and a Bachelors degree in

Economics but, since my GPA is somewhat low, I decided to go for another major. I decided to major in Statistics, which will help me a lot with my Economics, but also will get me to be more marketable to get a higher salary.

Conclusion

Since I was born, I have had many disadvantages, first not having a father and then not having my papers. It is the disadvantages that have made me keep going forward. I'm an individual, no different from the rest of my people from Mexico coming here for a dream. A dream that seems blurry sometimes, but it's a dream to succeed and provide our families with a better future. I'm no different; the only difference is that I'm actually getting an education and know that if there is any way that I could help my family, it's through helping myself graduate from college.

Once I can help myself, I can help others. Sure, there are times when I help others; that is just my nature that I obtained from my mother. If you were to ask me, why am I still in college, why am I still here? You can ask me this question even when I'm sixty years old, and I would still give you the same answer. My answer is because my mother didn't abort me when my biological father asked her to do so. It is because of her unconditional love and her decision to raise me by herself; it is through her sweat and sacrifices that I am still here. She was the one that set the stepping stones to my success for the future. She was the one who raised me to be the man that I am today, and because she took care of me when I was little, it's my turn to take care of her.

Pedro

The Beginning

My life began on July 4, 1989, in a small hospital in Lazaro Cardenas, Michoacán, Mexico. After a couple of months of living in the city, my mother had to take me back to the "rancho" where we lived with my stepdad. As a child I was oblivious to the reality of the world and all the problems that we were going through, which I never thought of as problems because I was used to living with them. I was a happy kid who thought that working at the age of six was something normal that every kid did at that age, which is somewhat true for many kids in Mexico, because they have to help their parents by having to generate some sort of income.

As a kid I simply followed the rules that were given to me, and I tried my best to do as well as my parents expected of me because, if I didn't,

I would either get a beating or I wouldn't be allowed to eat dinner for that day. Needless to say, at a young age I had to be a quick learner and know how to properly follow rules and orders in order to satisfy my parents. This routine went on for most of my youth until the age of nine. This year was the year in which I experienced most of the change that I went through as a kid.

This is the time in which my mother one day came up to me and told me that she would be leaving "para el norte," meaning to the United States in a couple of months. What was most surprising was that she actually gave me the choice to either go with her or stay with my "father." At an age of nine it was one of the hardest decisions that I would have ever made, and I'm sure that even at my current age it would be a difficult decision. When she asked me this question, I decided that I was going to stay because I thought I was happy and I wanted to live with my father, but later that same week I thought it over, and I found more reasons to leave with my mom than to stay.

The man that I considered my father at the time was a drug trafficker. He owned much land in which he grew different types of marijuana and sold it. He made my older and younger brother help him, even though we didn't know that what we were doing was wrong. He took advantage of us as kids, and, far worse, he took advantage of my mother. This is the main reason she decided to leave the country.

He was not only a drug trafficker, but he was nothing but trouble. He would beat her and beat us as well to the point that my mother got tired of it and decided that it wasn't worth it. She had to be strong and make a change for herself and, more importantly, for our future. Unfortunately she had to be even stronger in deciding who she brought with her because my "father" threatened her if she brought his son, our younger half-brother, with her, and he would make sure that none of us made it across. She could not sacrifice all of us, thus she decided to bring my older brother and me.

La Linea/The Line

The famous borderline was where we would be crossing into a whole new country. We would cross to the land of opportunity in which we would be able to be free from our past and start a new and better life. Though, simply crossing over the border is not as simple as it may sound because we were crossing as illegal immigrants. Unfortunately we could not afford to get a fake visa or passport or any identification of any kind to try and sneak our way in the safe way. We actually had to risk our lives in order to start a new life. I remember clearly getting dropped off by the bus that we took from

Michoacán. I'm not exactly sure where it was that we crossed, but we stayed with some family that we had. Two days later we met the coyote and paid him to cross us over. We left the house early in the morning and started walking the first steps of the long journey ahead of us.

That morning was a very cold morning, but as we continued to walk during the day it only got hotter and hotter. At the age of nine I did not realize the danger that I was in by crossing the border. But the coyote made sure he reminded us every step of the way by telling us to keep our heads down, to crawl here and often to run so that the border patrol wouldn't spot us and shoot us. As a nine year old it was very unnerving, thinking that if you were spotted you could get shot and killed, but this didn't stop us because we were already more than half way from making it to the magical "linea."

The day seemed to drag on forever, and the heat wouldn't go down. We began to get hungry, but we had no food because we could not afford to buy any after paying the coyote to cross us. One of the clearest memories I have of crossing was my mom while she ran. It was starting to get dark, and the night began to get cold. We were nearly at the end of our daylong, life threatening; life-changing journey, but my mom stopped walking. I went back for her and she said she was too tired and told me to go ahead without her.

At this point we were reaching some neighborhoods and lighted houses were coming up and the group began to jog the rest of the way. My mom urged me to catch up with them and to leave her behind. I knew I had to catch up with the rest of the group in order to make it across safely, but I couldn't leave my mom behind. I decided to stay and help her catch up with the rest of the group. I took her hand and started running as fast as I could and pulled her as hard as I could to get her to hurry. I knew that my mom, being as strong as she is, would find strength to make it in time before the group disappeared. And she did, she pushed herself and started running beside me as we ran toward the group, which had stopped to wait for us.

When we arrived to where the group was waiting, we were told to run into a hotel and hide in a specific room that was reserved for us, but to make sure we didn't get caught or that would be the end and our sacrifice would have been for nothing. Fortunately for us we made it in safely and we were greeted by a familiar face. One of our uncles was in the business of getting illegal immigrants into the states, and he met us there to take us the rest of the way to where our family was residing. This was the beginning of a new world and a new life.

A New Beginning

As you can imagine, for a kid, the whole ordeal, all of these past events, weren't sinking in. I never thought of it any different than me being in Mexico, and I still tried to be the same outgoing, over energized kid I was before. I did not go to school until a couple of months after getting to the country, and that's when I noticed the huge difference. The people were different, the way they acted was different, I was unable to communicate with them, and it was all a horrible feeling. I felt as if I didn't belong there and should be back in Michoacán, not in San Jose. For the longest time, the only reason I ever went to school was because my mom made me. She told me I had to go, otherwise I would have to leave the house for the night and sleep outside. This, of course, was just a threat to make me go to school, and it worked because I went to school every day. Being a quick learner, I learned the language very quickly and by then end of fifth grade I was able to have small conversations in English with other students, and I finally started to make friends.

Finding Myself in School, College, and the Future

As I grew up in a poor neighborhood and went to poor schools, I never had anyone tell me about going to college and getting good grades, so I didn't care much about school. I simply went because I was forced to. After my middle school graduation, I told my mom that I was going to look for a job and stop going to school, because I wanted to help my family. She knew that she needed the help, but she said to me, "Nada mas trata un año y si no te gusta te pones a trabajar." ("Just try it one year, and, if you don't like it, you can start working.") Once again, I simply went to my first year of high school because I wanted to please my mom and for no other reason. My ninth grade was the year in which my whole mindset of how to help my family changed. I originally thought that by getting a job I could help them out, but I never thought of going to college and getting a degree in order to get a better job.

The high school I went to held many workshops that explained to the students how college was a benefit for us and how we could help our families more by going to college instead of dropping out and getting a mediocre job that paid minimum wage. It was after this that I began to dedicate myself to the fullest and tried my best to get the best grades possible in all my classes. I became very involved in my school and took on positions in different clubs while also doing sports.

It was my junior year when I finally thought about what college I wanted to attend and how I was going to pay for it. That's when it hit me that I didn't have any money and I wasn't going to be able to apply for FASFA or other financial aid because they required a social security number, which I didn't have. It frustrated me to think that I tried so hard, got 4.0 GPA for three years and I wasn't even going to be able to go to college because I couldn't afford it.

Fortunately for me, I met with our high school counselor to ask if there was a way to pay for college fees. She gave me an extensive list of scholarship organizations that were willing to give money to students such as myself who were doing well in school and wanted to pursue their education. I applied to an unknown number of scholarships for almost a whole year. I didn't get any of them, and I thought I wasn't going to get any of them, but my senior year I got calls from different organizations that I had applied to. I managed to earn a total of $16,000 worth of scholarship money.

I am now in my second year in college through scholarships and my own work money. I have never received any government financial aid. I could not afford to pay even for rent if it wasn't for applying for all those scholarships. I consider myself very lucky to even be in college. There have been many times in which I thought about whether I will be able to afford college the next semester or not. For example, I am currently working thirty hours a week in order to save some money for next semester because I fear I might not get saved by any scholarships next time.

This shouldn't be the things that I think about. I should be thinking of when I will graduate and the things that I need to do to get there, not whether I'm even going to be in college in a year. Though my life has been hard, so has the lives of my mother and many others who share similar experiences, but we all still remain hopeful that one day things will change for the better and we will receive help in our endeavors.

PART III

Linda

Mi Mexico/My Mexico

I was born in a convent called "El Refuguio" or "the refuge" in Guadalajara, Jalisco. From what I am told it is a beautiful, colorful city in Mexico. It is also the birthplace of Mariachi. I don't remember what the city looks like because my parents brought me to the U.S. at the tender age of five years old. What I do remember is that my two younger brothers and I ran around barefoot because we had no money for shoes. My parents would go to the local market and ask the owner if they could please take some food, and pay him back sometime later. My father could not get a decent paying job.

At my young age, times were not so great in the beautiful city of Guadalarajara. My birthplace did not seem like much of a refuge. My father decided that it was time to go to "Los Estados Unidos" or the United States of America. I was excited, but I remember seeing tears run down my mother's face when she said goodbye to her mother, my grandmother. At the time, I didn't know that I would no longer see my sweet "mamI chui," the name I called my grandma. I also didn't know that I would never see the vibrant city that I used to call home. Well, at least I haven't yet.

Llegando a Los Estados Unidos/Getting to the United States

My father, Leopoldo Sanchez, was the second youngest of thirteen children. My mother was also one of the youngest children of six kids. Many of my uncles and aunts on both sides of the family were already in the United States. So, once we arrived it would not be difficult to find someone we could stay with until we got on our feet. The problem my father faced was how he was going to go about getting his wife and three kids to the U.S.

Leopoldo had worked in the States before he married my mother. He had crossed over illegally but had managed to get some sort of permit to work. For a while he worked here while the rest of us lived in Mexico. He would send money to my mother, but it wasn't enough. My mother would say, "*todos aqui o todos alla*," which basically meant that she wanted her family together in one place. She did not care where as long as we were together. My dad decided that "alla" or "over there" (in the United States) was better.

My father went about trying to find a way to get us all over here. One of his friends owned a hotel in Guadalajara. He asked this friend to lie and say that my dad worked for him and made a decent salary. Immigration only gave family visitor visas to people who had good paying jobs. These were only good for a few months, but we would overstay the visas; we just needed a way in. My dad borrowed money from one of his brothers so he could afford the five train tickets to Tijuana. From there we would have to cross the border in a truck. My mother's brother, my uncle Jorge, would get us across in his truck.

El Cruce/The Crossing

"El cruce" or the crossing was very nerve wracking. Although I was five, I knew very well what was going on. My brothers were very oblivious but my heart was racing. We had visitor visas, but my parents were so afraid of the "migra" or border patrol that they did not want to be questioned at all. They thought that the "migra" was more likely to stop them if we had too many people in the truck. The best way for us to not look suspicious was to have my uncle and my dad in the front (since they spoke some English). My mother, my brothers, and I were to lay as quiet as we could in the bed of the truck. It had a shell with tinted windows so one couldn't really see in.

My parents did not want to take chances with one of us kids making noise, so they gave us sleeping pills. I pretended to be asleep, but I remember staying awake the whole time. Later, in college, I would learn that sleeping pills make some people stay up (including me). I remember seeing bright lights through those dark camper shell windows. I also heard people speaking a really funny language. It almost sounded like all the strange words were slurred together.

Los Estados Unidos/The United States

The first place we lived in was a garage in El Monte, California. It is located in Los Angeles, and to my surprise there weren't any angels there. The summers were extremely hot, and my brothers and I were not allowed to play outside. My parents were afraid that someone would realize that we lived there and deport us. At one point there was a gas leak in the garage, and my mother, brothers, and I almost died. My dad got home from work just in time.

School was not what I had expected. I was extremely shy, and I could not speak any English. It seemed so hard, and I thought I was never going to learn it. I was the oldest child, so I did not have any older siblings who could help me with homework. My mom couldn't help me either because she did not know the language. My father was always too busy working. Kids at school made fun of me, and I had no friends. My family moved around a lot, so there was no time to make any friends. Even the food seemed strange. I had never had tater tots or spaghetti.

Every time my mom dropped me off at school, I would cry my heart out. I also missed my mami chui very much. Everything in Los Estados Unidos seemed very strange. All I wanted to do was go back to Mexico and not go to these crazy schools. I wanted to hug my grandmother. Before I went to bed I would pray that I'd go back to Mexico soon, but that never happened. One day I asked my mom if God only spoke English in the U.S.; maybe that was the reason he never answered my prayer.

A Young Lady

As a child one doesn't realize that one is poor. It is later that one notices that your family has incredibly less things than everyone else. I grew up in the city of Orange near Los Angeles. I had never had my own room or even a bed. I slept on the floor in front of the fireplace, this way I wouldn't get cold in the wintertime. We always lived in a tiny area, causing everyone to be crowded. Our cars also looked like they had escaped from a junkyard.

In high school I started realizing many things. I started going to friend's houses, and they all had their own rooms and had lots of food. The hardest thing that I had to do was come to grips with the fact I was undocumented. That is when it really hit me. It would not be that easy to get a job. How could I possibly get a job if I did not have the correct paperwork?

Luckily for me, when we came to the United States in 1989 immigration issued a social security number to anyone. My parents got all of us social security numbers. However, our cards read "NOT VALID FOR EMPLOYMENT." With this card I was able to get a driver's license. I was very fortunate to get one because I know plenty of people that do not have one.

When I went looking for a job I got a fake social security card in Santa Ana that did not say "NOT VALID FOR EMPLOYMENT." It had my real legitimate number on it, but it did not look too good. One of my first jobs was at Disneyland. I was hired. But, when they asked for all the documentation. I faced a huge problem. They turned my fake social security card and me away. I just cried and cried and cried and cried some more in my car.

Someone gave me the idea of erasing the "NOT VALID FOR EMPLOYMENT" of my real card, I did that and it worked! I worked for Mickey Mouse at the happiest place on earth for five years. I worked there my senior year of high school and all the way through community college. College was another eye opening experience to the harsh reality of my legal status.

College

Why do you want to go to college anyway? You are a woman, and as a woman you are just going to get married and have kids." This was my father's response when I told him that I wanted to go to a four-year university. He was okay with me going to trade school, but he thought college would take "too long." Besides, in his eyes, school was not really a women's place. Years earlier, he had not allowed my mother to go to English school.

I decided that I was not going to be like my mother and be obedient to the man of the house. I also made up my mind that I was not going to be another statistic. I did not want to be like many young Mexican women, who do not further their education. Most of the people I went to high school with did not go on to college. For me, getting an education was a way of rebelling against my father, rebelling against Mexican female norms, and the only way to escape poverty.

I could not afford to go to a university right away because that would have been too expensive. I attended Orange Coast College in Costa Mesa for four years while working full time at Disneyland. Although my family and I were poor, I could not receive financial aid because I was undocumented. My grades were outstanding but I did not qualify for many scholarships. Most scholarships require that you show proof of financial aid application. You can't apply for that or student loans if you are not legally here. Once again the unforgiving reality of my legal status was biting me in the butt.

In spite of all this, I was very thankful. I was very thankful for the sheer fact that I had a chance to go to college. Statistics show that only about 1 percent of the world's population gets a college education. In many countries women aren't even allowed to pursue a formal education. Thanks to the AB540 form, I was able to go to college and not pay out of state tuition fees. The AB540 form allows students who did high school in the United States to go to college.

After going to Orange Coast College for four years, I was accepted into a CSU Southern California campus. About 50,000 applied, and they only took 4,000 freshmen and 4,000 transfer students. This was a huge accomplishment for me. The day I received the acceptance letter was one of the happiest days of my life. Although my father did not like the idea of me going to school at first, his mind began to change when I was accepted. I think he began to realize that I was serious and very determined.

I had no idea how I was going to pay for college, or where I was going to live. But that is just the kind of person I am: sink or swim. I never really stop to think of all the obstacles in my way. I think people stop pursuing their dreams because they stop to think of all the things that could possibly go wrong. My father began to have a more positive view of school, and my mother and I took advantage of that. We persuaded him to let me borrow the money for school. He was able to do this by refinancing our house.

Two years seemed to fly by and on May 18, 2007, I graduated from a CS University with a Bachelor's in Anthropology. This was by far one of the happiest days of my life. When my name was announced I probably had more people cheering for me than anyone else graduating that day. I was the first one in my family to get a college degree. I just hope I can be an example to my younger brothers, cousins, nephew, and niece.

Post-graduate

Life after graduating was not really what I expected. I was going to apply for a translating job for the FBI. It paid good money, but then I realized that they do a very extensive background check. My friend said that if one is a "mojado" or wetback, it was best not to apply. She was right, and I decided to become a substitute teacher and tutor instead. Once again a reminder of my legal status was making itself evident and was frustrating to me. What good is a degree if I can't get a good paying job?

I decided that I would do something extremely crazy and desperate at this point. I decided to ask one of my guy friends if he would marry me so that I could become a citizen. We had been friends for over ten years and I decided, "Oh what the heck." One night I finally worked up all the courage and asked him. I don't really like to talk about the outcome. Let's just say that things did not go as planned, and I was completely humiliated. That's the last time I ask a dumb guy to marry me!! It's his loss, not mine. Besides I would want a guy to ask me, not the other way around.

Before I ever decided to ask that bozo what I had asked him I also decided that I wanted to get my master's and eventually my Ph.D. as well. I applied to a CSU campus again because they have an excellent anthropology master's program. It is #1 in California and one of the top ten in the United States. Over 100 people apply each year and they only accept eight to twelve. Once again I was accepted into school, and I was beyond happy.

The question of how I was going to afford school comes up once more. I am applying for a few scholarships that don't require you to be documented. I think that my mother and I might be able to convince my father to let me borrow at least some of the money for my tuition. It also helps that he is in a good mood. My mother and dad just received their residencies. It took about twenty years, but they finally got them. Unfortunately, my brother, Leo, and I will not get anything because we are over eighteen.

The Future

My parents and brother, Max, are legal residents of the United States now. With their new status, my mother and father have put in paperwork for Leo and me again. Immigration told them that it would take at least three more years for us to get our residencies. However, I don't believe that at all; I believe that it will take much longer than that. They give you a certain time, but it always takes years longer than what they say. That is just the way the system works, no matter how fair and easy anybody makes it seem on TV.

Although I might get something from immigration in the future, that will make me legal here, Leo will not. He has had a few run-ins with the law and is now facing deportation. ICE is deporting undocumented people with criminal records. My brother has broken the law, but I don't think he deserves to be deported. I know countless individuals that have done crimes way worse than what Leo has done, and they just got a little slap on the hand. My brother has not even been to Mexico since we left. It is going to be a strange world for him, I am not sure when I will see him again.

I hope that I will someday become legal in this country, and then I will be able to visit my brother. Hope is one thing, and reality another. I once asked an immigration lawyer the steps I could take in order to become legal in this country (this was before my parents became residents). She said, "You have to marry a citizen or have a child born here." It is obvious that the system in place now simply just does not work.

My Point of View

I believe that being a Mexican illegal alien woman has helped shaped my reality. This is both a good and a bad thing, and sometimes I feel that my reality is skewed. It is a good thing because it has helped me be cautious on an everyday basis. For example, I am very careful about who I tell that I am undocumented. It is not part of a regular conversation with friends at lunch. Most of my friends don't know that I am here illegally. I think that the less people who know about it, the better. That will make the chances of me getting deported a lot smaller.

It has also been bad in shaping my reality in several different ways. Being an immigrant Mexican young woman has allowed me to view many things first hand. There are some Hispanic men (but not just Hispanics) that are driven by machismo and beat their wives. I was unfortunate enough to see my father beat my mother repeatedly. I think this is not as predominant in second-generations Mexicans who have been more Americanized. I know that not all Latino men are like this and that husbands from other cultures beat their wives too. Nevertheless, I feel a deeper attraction to white men. I think that this is due in part of my fear of ending up with a guy who abuses me. Also, I know my dad would prefer I marry a Mexican. So, again, if I do the opposite, I would be rebelling against my father. I like the sound of that.

I am aware that my reality is a little off. This is never more apparent to me then when I cross the San Clemente checkpoint. The first time I crossed it, I was very nervous. However, after crossing a few times, it became normal. But when I cross, I can't help but think that they have a type of machine that can listen to anything that you are saying in your car. When I approach the checkpoint, I only listen to English music and don't talk in Spanish on my cell. I get the feeling that if I was listening to Vicente Fernandez, they would hear it on their machine and pull me over.

I am fully aware that these fears have no valid arguments, but they are there in my mind. In fact my family is a little afraid for me too. When I first moved to San Diego, my father said that I could not visit them in Orange County. He was sure that I would get caught at the checkpoint and get deported. My aunt and mother had me call them each time that I crossed the checkpoint to make sure I was okay. I no longer worry when I cross there anymore. In life I have realized that worrying is not going to protect me from deportation, get me anywhere, or change my legal status (or that of my brother). I have learned that I can only concentrate on goals and do my best.

My Goals

I will start my anthropology master's program in the beginning of September. I propose to do my thesis on developing a way to help Mexican immigrant children achieve higher education levels. I plan to keep working as a substitute teacher and as a tutor. I believe that by being an educator, I can help open the minds of many students. I want to keep going to school after my master's and get my Ph.D. My goal is to be a cultural anthropology professor someday. After receiving my Ph.D., I would like to help immigrants through research that will improve cultural understanding and educational standards.

I decided that I wanted to be a professor of anthropology for many reasons. Anthropology is the study of mankind through time and space. I believe that there is much one can learn from this field. It shows us that we are all the same, members of one single human race. Much of the world's hate stems from our inability as a species to have tolerance for our cultural differences. Anthropology opens our eyes and teaches us to question ideas that have been engraved in our minds to be perceived as facts and reality.

As part of my goals, I would like to someday visit Guadalajara. Well, that is a wish more that a goal. I have seen its beauty in postcards many times, but I want to see that colorful city with my own two eyes again. It has been twenty years since I last saw "mi Mexico," but I can still hear the mariachi at the plaza.

Conclusion

Although I would like to visit Mexico soon, I am thankful that I grew up here. I am thankful for all the opportunities that Los Estados Unidos has given me. I hope that in the future I will be able to help other immigrants grasp the opportunities that lay before them. These opportunities may not seem so apparent at first and are not that easy to grasp, but they are there. We can all be successful. In conclusion, I would like to quote Marianne Williamson. I love this quote because it puts into words the fact that all people have what it takes to be successful.

> *"Our deepest fear is not that we are inadequate. Our deepest fear is that we are powerful beyond measure. It is our light, not our darkness, that most frightens us. We ask ourselves, who am I to be brilliant, gorgeous, talented and fabulous? Actually, who are you not to be? You are a child of God. Your playing small doesn't serve the world. We were born to manifest the glory of God that is within us. It's not just in some of us; it's in everyone. And as we are liberated from our own fear, our presence automatically liberates others."*

> —Marianne Williamson

Norma

My Parents' Struggle

It makes me extremely proud to say that I was the first person in my family to graduate high school and to even attend college. I am currently a junior at a CS University, but getting here hasn't been so easy. I am the oldest of three children in my family and was brought to the United States at the age of nearly three years old. I was born in Leon Guanajuato, Mexico, a very culturally rich city where my entire family is from.

My parents met at a very young age, and they welcomed me to the world when they were only nineteen years old. My father Manuel came from a very poor family. He lived in a small house with both his parents and ten brothers and sisters. My mother Leticia grew up with a single mom and four brothers. Neither of them was lucky enough to receive an education because they couldn't afford it and, as my father jokes, school was something he didn't enjoy.

My parents endured the hardships of life at a very young age. My mother lost her father at the age of fifteen because of alcohol abuse, and, being the only daughter, she had to care for her brothers all her life. My father began working as a child to help support his large family. Their hard work and struggle to survive began early on in life. A year after I was born my father decided to try his luck in the United States. He would hear stories from people convincing him that life in America was easy and well paid. Since both he and my mother wanted a better life, they agreed that he should cross the border and test out his luck.

Shortly after he left my mother and family, I began to get sick. I was sick to the point of nearly dying. My mother would take me to the doctor to see if I could be diagnosed with something, but no one seemed to know what I had. Until one day, my mother came across a doctor who encouraged her to reunite me with my father. He claimed I was overwhelmed by his departure, and so my mother asked my father to come back. He did so in a heartbeat and when I had my father back in my life, no one could believe the quick recovery I had. My mother thinks it was a way of God letting us know that we couldn't be apart.

A Time for Change

Shortly after our family was reunited, my brother Guillermo was born. Within a year as soon as Guillermo turned a year old, my parents found themselves in a desperate need for change. My father was working full time as a shoemaker and my mom would sell clothes. Even though they both contributed to the household, it still wasn't enough. My father knew that his experience in the United States hadn't been easy, but he learned from experience that jobs in America helped pay the bills. He wanted to return, but was afraid that either my brother or I would feel his absence, so he convinced my mother to migrate as a family.

At first, my mother was skeptical she didn't want to leave her homeland, but she knew America would open up doors, especially for my brother and me. She also wanted to come because her mother, my grandmother, had already established a life in the United States. So it was decided that my mother, brother, and I would first travel and get settled and then my father would follow us in a few weeks because he needed to take care of unfinished business back home. It's as though he had a feeling he would never get to come back and see his own parents.

My mother's uncle Gabriel was the leader of our group. He had migrated many times to the U.S. and knew his path through the desert, so he decided to help us cross. The group consisted of my mother, brother, my uncle Angel, his seven-month-pregnant wife Laura, and I. There are times when I have memories of my journey as if they were dreams or a déjà vu, but most it is the recollection of the story from my family's perspective.

My uncle Gabriel carried me the entire time, and my uncle Angel was carrying my brother. My mother would help my aunt Laura because of her pregnant condition. We traveled through the desert for an entire day. I remember being very tired, thirsty, and most of all scared because there were times when everyone would run or hide. My mother remembers me questioning everything we did. I could not understand the reasons why we were doing that.

Our Arrival

My uncle Gabriel had carried a bag of clean shirts because he knew that as soon as we were on American ground we needed to change in order to not attract attention. And that is exactly what we did. As soon as we crossed we changed clothes, cleaned our shoes, and began to walk as casual as possible. A few minutes later, a border patrol vehicle passed by us and maintained a close watch.

My mother recalls making my brother and me laugh as though we were taking a walk in the park. My uncle helped my pregnant aunt and made sure it was obvious she was due any day now. It was important for them to pretend we were ordinary people. Fortunately, we were not detained and deported that day. Eventually, we made our way to my grandmother's one bedroom home where we all lived for a period of time. My aunt gave birth to my cousin about three weeks after arriving.

My father had worked as a landscaper with a man he met during his first stay in the United States. Once he arrived for the second time, my uncle Gabriel recommended him to work at a body shop where he knew the owner. He was promised a salary of one hundred dollars a week but was later only paid eighty. My father did not complain because he knew it was a much better salary than what he was earning in Mexico. He was able to afford things he couldn't before.

My father slowly began to learn more about his job and realized he was being taken advantage of. He then began to look for another job and found the one he has now. We were able to move out of my grandmother's home as soon as my father began to work. A few years later my youngest brother was born, making him the only one to have legal documentation. Through the years we moved several times from home to home, but always found ourselves staying in the same neighborhood.

Growing Up

I mostly grew up in Logan Heights where my brothers and I were surrounded by bad influences all around. Gangs, drugs, and violence were a typical thing in my block. People would vandalize your house or break into your cars. There were a few times we would wake up to find our vehicles stolen. Most crimes would go unreported because of the fear of being questioned by police or being turned over to immigration. Also, border patrol agents were constantly seen on the streets. I lived half a block away from a market, and, every time my mom needed something she would send my brother and me to get it for her, but she would ask us to first check that immigration wasn't there. If they were, we had to return home immediately and as a child I did what I was told without realizing the logic behind it.

As I grew older I began to hate immigration and think of them as people who were out to get us for no reason. The constant checkpoint made my parents nervous because they knew that at any moment they could easily get pulled over and lose everything they had worked for. I knew that we had done no harm and yet we were being criminalized. I saw a lot of depressing things where I lived and people who did not care about going to school or making something out of their lives. I knew I wanted something better for the sake of my family and myself and because of that, ever since I can remember I wanted to learn and accomplish something in my life.

My Academic Years

I was able to start school in the United States at an elementary school. Ever since I can remember I liked school. I was always a good student and got good grades. All my teachers saw potential in me, and they encouraged me to always work hard. When I was in middle school I met two teachers who changed my life. In the seventh grade I met Ms. Amy. She was my AVID teacher. She encouraged me to apply for a scholarship from the San Diego Padres, and after a long process I was given five thousand dollars for a four year institution. It was then, that I realized that college was something I could stop dreaming about and actually accomplish regardless of my legal status. In the eighth grade I met my history teacher Mr. Chavez. He also influenced my life because he had helped me achieve so much and has guided me through some of the most difficult situations in my life.

Throughout high school I continued to get good grades and decided to really get involved in school, which is where I learned how I could make it to college. AVID provided me good information and my counselor at the time knew my entire story, because he was the only person who was able to communicate with my parents. He began helping me with both school and my legal case. In the twelfth grade I decided that even though my legal case in becoming a legal resident wasn't moving forward, I still had to continue school.

I found out that four year colleges where accepting students despite being illegal. Among my friends only three of us applied to schools throughout California. I had a friend who was in the same position as me, but refused to accept the possibility of going to college that she decided not to apply. When I got my acceptance letter from three of the four universities I had applied to, I was the happiest person. I strongly believed that I was college bound. College life, however, brought with it many unexpected trials.

I was accepted and chose to attend a CS University. While being able to pay for my initial year of college, I struggle to pay for my expenses, such as books, transportation, and lunches. My college experience has been the most challenging time of my life. I have been able to grow, but at the same time I've had to go through really difficult things. When I began my college career, I was consider an AB540 student, meaning that because I had attended and graduated from a high school in the United States I would not be charged out-of-state tuition. The only disadvantage is that I did not qualify for financial aid. I've had to juggle both a full time job and be a full time student. I have also had to deal with legal matters that have greatly affected my entire family.

The Continuing Struggle

In January of 2007 my mother received a letter from the district attorney's office stating she was being charged with three felonies because she used false documentation to obtain a job. As usual, she took it as casual things, but I knew that the problem wouldn't go away that easily. She was set to attend court a month later, and there she was told that she could be booked and perhaps released at the women's detention facility in Santee, California, known as Las Colinas.

When she did so, she was detained by ICE and held for about two days before my family was able to provide the bail for her. Thereafter, a series of never-ending court appearances proceeded. We had to get a lawyer, who ended up taking advantage of us. He did nothing to help my mother; instead his actions landed her in jail one more time, but this time for nearly a month in late August of this year. Our new lawyer worked really hard and was able to get the charges against my mother dropped.

Looking into My Future

I will receive my Bachelors degree in May of 2009. My plans are to attend the teaching credential program and pursue my passion for teaching. When I think about this goal of mine, I feel a sense of happiness because I'm very close to achieving it, but then my happiness quickly turns to sadness. The road to my goal becomes blocked. Given my status, I will not be able to teach. The process to become a teacher consists of a background check through a fingerprint screening process; I can't even complete the initial step of providing my social security number. I constantly find myself extremely frustrated and angry about my reality, and the obstruction of my goals. I hear and see horrible teachers who do not help their students become successful, and I think to myself how I would love to help students and see them grow as individuals. If only I had the opportunity.

PART IV

Diego

Where to begin? How to begin? For years my voice has been silent and un-heard. To many, my words have no power or meaning. Like me, there are many others who have lost their voices and whose stories haven't been told. I am one of many, living in the shadows of American society. A *foreigner* caught in a system where "barriers" are built day after day, barriers which seem to be created to prevent success, built to keep us from reaching our goals and unleashing our potential. It is time to speak in a unified voice so our stories can be heard. It is time for hope that someone listens to us and understands what it is to live in constant fear, and the struggle to achieve goals. Living each day in constant fear that you might lose everything you have accomplished, and living in the shadows trying to pass unnoticed.

The Push Factor

I was born to a well-educated and economically stable family. My father was a university graduate from a recognized medical school. He struggled to pay for his own career, oftentimes suffering hunger and working long shifts in order to afford tuition and expensive books during the six years of study, not counting the first year service that had to be done after graduating from medical school. After some years of hard work and savings, he managed to build his own house, a doctor's office, his own electronics' store, and was able to support a family of five. He was even able to afford the costly price of private school for my older brother and me to go to a private Catholic elementary school. We were the top students of our classes every year from kindergarten through sixth grade.

Everything seemed to go well until the year of bad political decisions, which affected many Mexicans and made them lose all, if not everything they had. This period was known to many as the 1994 economic crisis in Mexico, where the "Mexican peso" was devaluated, which led many businesses to go bankrupt. Many homeowners were left without a roof to shelter their families, and many of those affected by this economic crisis often resorted to suicide.

I was a kid back then, and I did not understand the gravity of the situa-tion. I didn't know what had occurred with my dad's business, why we were receiving calls from the bank every day, and why we were also at risk of los-ing our house. All I was told was that we were going to leave the country to live in the United States, learn English, and visit Disneyland. After hearing we were going to Disneyland, I thought it would be a happy and pleasant stay in the United States and hurried back to my room to pack my belongings. I still remember the morning after when I realized I had to leave my extended family, my friends, and my pets, which were like my best friends.

Everything I knew was to be left behind. I spent all day crying and worrying about the well-being of my pets, which was more like a zoo. We had dogs, turtles, birds, fishes, chicken, sheep, and, many more. Luckily for me, my parents were really good at making me believe things; they would calm me down and convinced me all animals were going to be fine. A few months passed until we were given the U.S. tourist visa. My family sold most of our belongings, some were given away to people in need, and we continued to prepare for our departure. My brother and I stayed with my grandparents for a couple of months in central Mexico, while my mom and little sister went to Ensenada, Baja California, to stay with her brother. Meanwhile my father went to Los Angeles with some friends whom had offered him a job.

My mom chose Ensenada because it was closer for my dad to go visit my mom. It was a three-to-four-hour drive from Los Angeles to Ensenada, and we didn't know anyone in northern Mexico except for my uncle. My parents knew it would be easier for us to cross to the U.S. once my dad had saved enough money for an apartment. Two months later my brother and I arrived in Ensenada to reunite with my mom and sister.

A Un Paso de la Frontera/One Step Away from the Border

My dad's job was not well-paid, and due to his legal status, the jobs paid low wages to illegal workers. This made our stay in Ensenada longer than expected. My dad was only able to send us enough money monthly to rent an apartment and buy a short supply of food. We made the groceries last the whole month even if it meant eating twice or even once a day. Dessert was out of the question, and drinking soda was a privilege we couldn't afford, so we always drank tap water which tasted badly. We only had a small black and white TV that for some reason only would show *novelas,* which to this day I still hate. My toys and clothes were bought in *Las Segundas,* thrift shops, where poor people shopped.

Thanks to some of my uncle's friends we were able to enroll into a public middle school and have our school uniforms for free, same with my little sister who was enrolled in a kindergarten nearby our apartment. One thing I hated about school was the distance; it was about six miles from where we lived. Most of the times I had to walk to and from school because I didn't have the three pesos (about 30 U.S. cents) for the bus fare. School was not a good experience for me, given that I was always picked on by other students because of my southern accent. All of a sudden my academic achievement went down to average, and I found it hard to focus on my classes. I knew it was partly due to poor nutrition, but it was mainly the lack of presence of my dad that made it hard for me to keep my mind in school.

It was hard not having Dad around. My older brother and I never talked about it, but my little sister reminded us every day that we needed him. Whenever my dad came to visit, we would have the best time, hoping his stay would be longer, but at the end of the day he had to go back to Los Angeles. This would sadden all of us. I still have vivid images of my little sister crying and yelling to my dad, *"Papi no te vayas, no nos dejes,"* which means, "Daddy, don't go, don't leave us." We noticed it broke my dad's heart to see my little sister like that, but it was only a matter of time until we were living together again.

My uncle's wife (we never called her aunt for personal reasons) oftentimes tried to talk us out of going to live in the U.S., not because she was worried for us, but because she was the type of person who never accomplished anything in her life and did not like seeing others succeed. She used to tell my mom that all schools in the U.S. were full of gangs and drugs, and if she were to take us there, we would become gangsters and drug addicts. Regardless of all the negative comments and the little support, my parents were determined to try, to give us a better life and a good education in order to succeed in life.

One day, our neighbor Chabelita came to the apartment and invited my mom to go shopping with her in Chula Vista. I remember that day because she brought us cookies and milk which were delicious. After a small chat with Chabelita, my mom agreed to go with her to Chula Vista the following morning while my brothers and I were in school. When I came back from school I saw a smile in my mom's face, so I thought that she had bought us some toys or American food, but the only thing she brought us was a bag of candy, and one box of cereal, Fruity Pebbles, if I'm not mistaken. But that wasn't the reason for her smile; she told me she had great news.

Thanks to the help of one of my uncle's wife's relatives who lived in Chula Vista, my mom was able to find a job for my dad. This meant he would be closer to us and could visit more often. Dad called us that same night and my mom told him she found him a job and he needed to go to Chula Vista as soon as possible. My dad arrived early the next morning and took my mom with him for the interview. They came back late at night and woke us up for even greater news. It turned out that my uncle's wife's niece was the manager of an apartment complex; she offered my dad a job and said she could rent us an apartment regardless of our legal status in the U.S. She understood our situation and wanted us to live together. They even helped my mom with all the school paperwork, all we had to do was show up to school. I still thank them to this day for their help and giving us the opportunity of renting a place so we could all be together.

We were anxious to leave Ensenada and to finally be together, hoping the change would give us an easier life. Our family was full of dreams and hopes, we thought everything would be easier living in the U.S., and we understood it would require many sacrifices from all of us. It took us a week to sell and give away some of the furniture we had in Ensenada, the only things we took with us was the small black and white TV, some blankets, pillows, and our clothes.

La Llegada al Otro Lado/Arriving on the Other Side

It was mid-February when we arrived in Chula Vista. The apartment was small for a family of five, but the good thing was that it was almost twice the size of the Ensenada apartment. We were happy to have a place to be together regardless of the small-sized apartment. We also did not have any furniture, except for a chair we found that day in the dumpster. Nevertheless it felt like home once again, no more living apart, no more crying, and no more being sad.

My dad only had a few dollars left because he had to pay the month's rent in advance, so he told us we were going to have to wait until he had enough money to buy us a bed, a dining table and chairs. We got used to the idea of sleeping on the floor, and eating on the floor as well.

The first night in the apartment was hard for me, and I'm sure it was for my parents and brothers also. My brain was not able to shut down that night, my eyes couldn't close, and all I could think about was what the future held for me in this new country. A huge list of "what ifs" came to mind, What if I don't make any friends? What if they make fun of me in school? What if I can't learn English? What if I don't like this country? What if . . . ?

When my brain finally stopped creating those useless thoughts and doubts, I noticed the sunlight entering through the window and heard my mom yelling "Ya despiertense!" I was already awake and it was time for school.

Primer Dia de Escuela/First Day of School

I still remember my first day of school in perfect detail. I arrived at the Castle Park Middle's main office and was taken to the counselor's office for my class schedule. The counselor spoke only English; since I didn't understand a word he was saying, I just nodded my head as if I understood. He gave me a piece of paper and pointed me to the door. I didn't know what all those numbers meant, room number, first period, second period, nutrition break, advisory, and so on. The school system was different than Mexico's school system, and my lack of English, made it difficult to find out where I was supposed to go. All I could say in English was my name, please and thank you. I thought everyone in the school spoke English only, because the two Hispanic looking guys I asked for help didn't understand me or maybe they refused to help me.

I was on the verge of tears when a teacher asked me something I didn't understand, obviously in English, so I just showed him my class schedule and he was able to show me to my first classroom. I arrived late to class, and the minute I walked in I noticed the other students checking me out from head to toe. I knew they were going to make fun of me because of my old clothes, and I was right. By the end of first period I was already nicknamed "Chespirito," because of a famous Mexican T.V. show that took place in a poor neighborhood. Thanks to the help of other nice kids, I was able to find my way to the rest of my classes, they showed me where to get my lunch, which was the best part of the school day, and showed me where they ate.

During lunch time I sat with the other Mexican kids, I had never seen such various types of ethnic groups. I also noticed that they were all segregated. African Americans gathered on one side, Anglos were in the middle next to a few Asians, the Mexicans who refused to speak Spanish who were popular and thought of themselves as being non-Mexicans, and then us at the back of the school next to the Handball courts, the so called "Beaners." It all got clear why we were called that as the days passed by.

Almost every day I was picked on by the others because of my out-of-style clothes. I didn't wear baggy jeans; my parents didn't have money to buy me the new Jordans, all they could afford was the ten dollar sneakers at Walmart. I was simply not popular and had a hard time fitting in. The only thing I loved about school was the free breakfast and lunch for kids of low-income parents. I could eat pizza or a hamburger in school, a luxury that my parents wouldn't be able to afford. When I heard there would be a new school uniform policy for the following year I was so happy and relieved. Next school year began with uniforms being mandatory, I was still called

Chespirito, but at least I didn't have to worry about wearing my old rags to school and people laughing at my clothes.

Outside of school, there were more things to worry about. We were told by my parents not to talk to strangers, especially government officials. If we were asked our country of origin by neighbors, friends or simply anyone, we would have to say we were born in Los Angeles and that we had just moved to San Diego recently. My parents explained our situation in detail, the way we had to behave in order to keep away from trouble, and especially keep them out of trouble since they would have to answer if we did something wrong and could possibly face deportation. We had to be on our best behavior in school and outside of school too. We were afraid to open the door when we heard knocks on the door. My dad still drove his old car with Mexican license plates, and at times when going for a ride we would panic if we saw a border patrol vehicle on the road. We were told to act normal and not even turn our heads to see the vehicle. I also grew up with a fear of police officers. In a few words, we had to hide in a shadow and be invisible.

My teenage years were spent working and digging through dumpsters. I remember jumping in the apartment's dumpsters to find useful stuff such as furniture, house appliances, and also aluminum cans to recycle and sell, in order to make money so I could help my parents. I had so much fun digging through the dumpster; it was like a treasure hunt to me. I was eager to find something useful to give to my mom. Sometimes I found chairs that were almost new, since we always took turns to sit on the only chair we had. One day it would be my mom's turn to sit down while eating, and the next my dad's, and so on. I would find so many things in the dumpsters, such as sofas, dining tables, lamps, stuffed animals for my little sister, toys, or soccer balls. Almost the entire apartment was furnished with stuff from the dumpsters.

I was thirteen when I began working in a flower shop, and it was an easy job. I would sweep the floors, fill buckets with water, clean the roses by removing the thorns, etc. The owner of the flower shop was Don Meño. He was a generous man who helped my family a lot. He gave me small things to do in his shop and paid me for it. He tried to help us several times by giving us a new mattress, cups, plates, and candy. My dad worked for him sometimes when they needed him to drive, pick up flowers, or make deliveries. There is no doubt Don Meño is an angel who was sent to help us, and I will always be thankful for his aid.

My mom had a job cleaning apartments and houses, she was hired by a Puerto Rican lady who knew our situation and offered to help us. She paid my mom twenty-five to thirty dollars a day. My mom didn't know if that was good pay, but my mom took the job because we needed the money. On many occasions her boss would pay her a week or two late. Then one day she owed my mom a good amount of money, and we never heard from her again. House cleaning is a hard job; I saw the look on my mom's face when she came back from working eight to ten hours straight and still had strength to cook us dinner. I often went with her to help her clean the apartments, and I learned firsthand how tiring and exhausting that job is. A lot of people paid her very little for her job, and then there were more people who never paid her at all. It was sad for me to learn that there were people who were making profits through her hard effort and labor. They were taking advantage because of her legal status. It hurt me to know that those people didn't have a heart, and did not care about the families of their employees. Unfortunately, that continued to happen for some years, but that didn't keep my parents from working hard.

High School Years

My high school years were not any different than those of middle school. Things got harder for me, and now there were new phases in my life where I knew I would have trouble. Every teenager faces phases such as academics, fitting in with friends, dealing with peer pressure, and dating.

I was enrolled in the bilingual program in middle school, but now that I was going to start ninth grade, my parents didn't want me to take bilingual classes. They wanted me to enroll in all English classes. It was hard for me to fit in with all the other students and try to learn English so quickly. Now I was made fun of because of my accent, but that didn't stop me from learning English; it just encouraged me to improve it. My brother and I told my dad to buy us a TV that showed "Closed Captions," so every time we watched cartoons or shows, we would read what they were saying. Reading closed captions on T.V. really helped us both, and by the end of ninth grade, my English had improved significantly.

I began to take Advanced Placement (AP) classes; it was in tenth grade when I found out that I wasn't going to be able to attend college in the United States due to my legal status. All the A.P. and Honors classes I had taken, now seemed worthless and a waste of time. Since the day I found out that I couldn't go to college, my GPA decreased. I didn't see a point on getting good grades if I wasn't going to be able to continue my education. The counselors in Castle Park High School, showed little interest and did not keep us updated with new academic opportunities. Our school was known for having a bad reputation on academics. The school was in bad shape and was mostly known for being a troubled school, with fights breaking out almost every day.

My social life in school was not the greatest. I had a hard time fitting in with different groups. As the years went by, I learned to choose my friends. Some social groups required ditching school, and I was afraid of being caught by the police. Others required getting in fights, and I knew I couldn't get in trouble because my parents would be involved too. There were others who were known for drug dealing, and even though the money was tempting and would have helped me, my education and personal values taught by my parents kept me away from those types of people. Just like every other kid, I wanted to be popular and be part of the football team, I knew I could have been a great wide receiver; I had quick feet, great hands, and good height. But there was something I didn't have—the money to pay for the expenses and the time to train, since I had to work to make money and help my parents. I knew I couldn't ask my parents for money, money which I knew they didn't have, so I just continued to go the same way.

I wasn't able to find a girlfriend in school, not because I was ugly, or fat, but because you could only get the girl you liked if you were popular, and obviously I wasn't. However, I was able to date girls from other schools, and that made my life less miserable. By the end of tenth grade, my brother graduated from high school and his only option was to go to a university in Mexico. He was accepted there and now my dad had more bills to pay, since el Tec de Monterrey is a prestigious and expensive institution in Mexico. It was great news for the whole family, but I knew I had to work double because my dad would have many things to pay for, such as my brother's tuition, books, rent, and food expenses.

It was then when I heard about a club called BMG that sold twelve music CDs for the price of one, and gave you extra CDs for getting people into the club. I joined the club, got some people to join, and began selling CDs. I was making a profit selling them to the neighbors, and friends in school, I had a good clientele. I also told my mom to bake cookies and desserts, so that I could sell them. It was the necessity that made me learn about business. I noticed I was good at it, and from that moment I began to pay attention to economics class and business. Even though I made some money selling cookies, cheesecakes, and CDs, I knew I had to find a job. I was able to buy a fake Social Security card, and Resident Alien I.D. that said I was eighteen years of age. I was only seventeen, but I knew that I needed to be over eighteen to work without any complications.

I heard of a job opening at a restaurant; they were looking for a dish-washer, so I quickly went to apply. I got the job the same day I went to apply, and told my parents the news. I was used to hard labor, so I did my best, and thanks to my English I was moved to host, which was an easy job for me. I had to get used to being called by another last name, and I often ignored others when I was being called. After a few months I got used to it.

In my senior year I changed jobs, now I worked for a 99-cent store, un-loading, unpacking, and, racking merchandise. Graduation was approaching and I was ready to leave to Mexico and continue studying over there. I didn't go to the prom because it was expensive, and I knew my parents could use the money for something else instead of me going to a dance. I was used to missing out on the dances, and even though all my friends were excited and asking everyone else about prom, I had already made my decision on not going. Graduation finally arrived, and I was done with high school.

Thanks to my friend Roberto whom I met in the church's youth group, I found out about the Assembly Bill 540 (AB540), which made tuition afford-able for immigrant students. He was enrolled in college under the same bill, so he helped me fill out the paperwork and enroll in a community college. Thanks to his help, I stayed in the U.S. to study and did not go to Mexico. I still can't understand why my high school counselors never told me about this; they knew my situation and still never told me I could continue my education in the United States.

College Life

The first day I went to college I declared my major in International Business. I was good with numbers, understood basic economics, and I was a quick learner when it came to languages. It was a career that I was passionate about and it came natural to me. I was determined to learn as much as I pos-sibly could.

My first year of college was difficult; I had no idea of the fees for being a full-time student, the expensive price of books, and the long hours of study needed for each class. In order to pay my way through college I was pushed to find a second job, so I began working in a liquor store. I was working over forty hours a week between my two jobs, plus I was a full-time student. I wanted to attend summer school my first year, but I wasn't able to because I had to make money for next semester's fees and school supplies. By the end of my first college year, I had a low GPA and was put under probation, which meant that if I received a low GPA again I would be kicked out of school. The need of buying a car pushed me to work more hours and get a third job.

I went to school on Mondays, Wednesdays, and Fridays from 7 to 11 A.M., one class right after the other. Then I would work from 12 to 5 P.M. and then start my other job from 6 to 11 P.M. Tuesdays and Thursdays I worked my third job from 1 to 7 P.M. and sometimes till later if it was busy. I had little time to rest and to do homework. On top of that I had a new girlfriend, so I was not 100 percent devoted to school. I had a bad relationship with my girlfriend, and she even threatened to call the immigration on my family if I didn't do what she wanted one day. Thanks to God, we broke up and I never saw her again.

The following semester I found a letter in the mail, it was the letter I had feared to receive. It was to inform me that I had been kicked out of college for low academic accomplishment, and I couldn't attend next semester unless I petitioned for reinstatement. I had to write an essay explaining why I had underachieved, the things I would change and explain why I deserved a second chance. Of course it still had to be authorized in order to be reinstated. I waited to see the results, and luckily I was allowed to go back.

The next spring semester I quit two jobs and was left with only one job in order to focus more on school. Only during summer I worked extra hours from Monday through Saturday at a car wash from 7 A.M. to 7 P.M. It was heavy work, cleaning 350 to 400 cars a day. My hands felt numb at the end of the day from the pressure of the water gun, and my shoulders felt heavy from brushing the cars. It was then when I realized school was a better option, and studying was what I needed to do to avoid those types of jobs. Like my grandpa used to say, "No hay mejor inversion, que invertir en tu educacion." There isn't a better investment, than investing in your education. So far he's been right; it has opened many doors and I'm better prepared.

At nineteen years of age I bought my first car, a '91 Ford Expedition. I saved enough money to buy it by not going out, no parties, no eating outside, and no shopping. It was an old car, but I was happy with it. Now I faced a new problem, acquiring my driver's license. I was afraid to cross to Tijuana and back to the U.S. even though I had my visa. The fear of Border Patrol agents finding out in their computers that I lived here always kept me from going to Tijuana frequently. I had to go to Ensenada to get my driver's license, and I figured it was better to have a Mexican driver's license than not having one at all. I had and still have the fear of being stopped by the police and being questioned about why I'm driving a vehicle with a Mexican driver's license. I have no other option but to drive like that, I must always be careful when driving and hope to God I don't get nervous if I ever get pulled over.

College involves socializing and partying frequently. Because most college students are under the age twenty-one, they tend to go to clubs in Tijuana. I was invited many times to go with friends there, and I only went a few times while my visa was still valid. I only crossed with a friend who knew about my situation and never told the rest of them about my legal status; they thought I was a U.S. citizen. Now that my visa expired, I make up excuses whenever I get invited to Tijuana, or Los Angeles, and at age twenty-three I still haven't been to Las Vegas. I am imprisoned, I can't go south, I can't go north, I can't go east, and to the west I have the Pacific Ocean. I'm surrounded by boundaries that stop me from visiting new places, barriers that have been with me since my arrival to the United States.

I graduated from a community college with an associate's degree in French, and another in Transfer Studies. I am currently a student at a CS University working to achieve my bachelor's in International Business, and a minor in Italian. Now I face a new challenge in my life. One, I must go to Mexico to study as a part of the International Business program; it is not an option, but a requirement. Two, if I graduate from the university, I will not be able to work here. I have thought about my options, and I'm willing to go back to Mexico and work over there as soon as I graduate if I can't work here in the U.S. I know that I need to take the risk of leaving the country to go study in Mexico and try to renew my visa, so that I can come back and finish my career. I'm only asking for an opportunity to finish my career and unleash my potential.

How do you tell someone who has worked and struggled all his life to achieve an education, that he simply cannot accomplish his goals? Why create more obstacles for the few that have walked a long journey? Why the interest in creating an educated society if the door of opportunity will not open for them?

Now I realize my potential, and hope that my voice gains volume. I want those shadows to become light, and their voices to unify. Just like me there are many others who have suffered injustice, rejection, worked hard day and night to achieve their goals, and no matter how big the barriers are, they still have the courage to fight and climb. The time is now, to have open ears, to see through our eyes, walk in our shoes and feel what we feel. It hasn't been easy for me or for my family and I hope people are conscious of the difficulties illegal immigrants face. I believe people will listen, understand and react. I have faith, and in faith there is always hope.

Roque

My name is Roque, I was born in Yucatan, Mexico on September 13, 1988. My father immigrated to this country in 1990. Two years later in 1992 I and my mother Guadalupe also immigrated here, I was only three years old. I have two younger sisters, both were born here. One is twelve years old, and my baby sister is seven months.

My father saved enough money to cross me and my mother into the U.S. I really respect and love my dad for caring enough for me and my mother when he could have easily continued his life in the U.S. by himself. My father was only eighteen when I was born and my mother was seventeen. My parents' hard work, determination, and humble spirit inspired me to reach a CS University.

My Awakening

I started school and my immigration status had not yet affected me. I played on youth soccer clubs, joined a karate class, and was always an honor-roll student. It wasn't until my sophomore year in high school that I found out I wasn't the same as all my other friends. At the time some of my friends were talking about getting their driver's license, getting a part-time job, and talking about their summer trips to other countries. I assumed I can do the same, so I asked my dad if I can get my license; that was when I realized my future was going to be filled with struggles, emotional pain, and disappointment.

I was too young to understand the legal system, but my parents would always tell me to get good grades, go to college, and nothing was ever going to stop me from doing what I wanted to do. I joined the junior varsity football team at my high school, and it seemed from that point on everything I did had to be different. All my teammates had medical insurance, and they would easily go to their private doctor to get physicals to be able to play. I remember how my mother and I had to shop around to get the cheapest price for a physical since I wasn't able to get medical insurance.

I started to have a lot of new friends at school as a result of being a football player, so I started going out more often and spending money. My parents never denied me money, but I have always been the type of person who doesn't like to spend money if it isn't mine. I would see many immigrant men such as my uncles and older cousins come back home dirty and tired from a long day of hard work and I would feel guilty asking for money since I would go out and spend it on myself and not with my family.

One time a couple of friends and I were going to a club in Hollywood to celebrate a friend's birthday. We stood in line for about twenty minutes just for me to get denied entry because I did not have a California I.D. I only had my Mexican I.D., and I was really mad because my I.D had my birthday and was also government issued. The club is also losing money, but I guess all that doesn't matter, since racism is still alive in that club. Luckily my friends that came with me also refused to enter, and if I one day I get legalized I would never go back to that club.

Not having a California I.D. has really had an impact in my life. Another incident occurred at Bally's. My friends and I were going to work out at that gym during the summer break, but in order for me to able to start a gym membership, I needed a California I.D. Unfortunately I couldn't start a membership; my friends felt really bad. I decided to work out at home, but what really made me frustrated was that I wasn't able to bond with my high school friends by sharing our college stories.

One time my dad told me that I deserve to have money to spend since I would always receive good grades, He said that was my only job was studying and I did it. He would tell me he doesn't care if he has to work three full-time jobs and have sleepless nights because he wanted to prove to me that my hard work does pay off, and one day I would go to college and have a professional career. I did not get a part-time job until I graduated high school; the interview was one of the most nerve-racking situations I have ever been in. While I worked I was always scared to mess up on the job in any way, because I thought that would be enough reason to review my background and possibly discover that I'm illegal. Fortunately everything worked out, and I was able to save some money for college.

My College Experience

By the time graduation approached, my plans were set. I was going to a CS University, and I was willing to sacrifice many things in order to achieve my dreams and make my family proud. I know I'm a huge role model for both of my sisters as well, and I can't even imagine disappointing them in any way. When I was applying to colleges, I was lucky enough to be covered by AB540, which allows me to pay in-state tuition, rather than out-of-state tuition which is more expensive. At the time my father was a co-owner of a rim company he and his friend had started. He sold his share of the company, and that was able to cover my freshman year fees, which included the highly expensive room and board expense. Since I couldn't receive financial aid, grants, or loans, my parents worked really hard to be able to cover the expensive costs of college.

It's really depressing to live life knowing I can't get a driver's license to drive back home and visit my family or take a girl out on a date without her having to drive, go to any club I want without the risk of getting denied entry, consider getting a loan when I have no money to eat normally at times, and be able to apply for a good job/internship regardless of the requirements. Nevertheless, I adjusted to living on campus and joined a fraternity. Not so long ago I filled out a form to apply for an internship. I made time from my busy schedule to attend the interview, and the interviewer liked my interview and called me back for a second interview where I would meet the president of the San Diego region of the internship. I was really excited; being a business major, I knew this internship was something I've wanted to do since my arrival to college. Unfortunately I was not given a chance to start the second interview because my application stated that I did not have a driver's license or a car, which was a mandatory requirement to qualify for the internship. I must admit I cried when I got home from the frustration and disappointment when I got denied acceptance due to something I couldn't control. My interviewer mentioned that only about 5 percent of students advance to the second interview with the president, this made me realize that they're willing to settle for a citizen less qualified over an immigrant who's more qualified.

One of the closest experiences I've ever had to possibly being deported was in April 2007. My fraternity had a nationwide event at Colorado State University, and we rented a van to road trip over there. We were stopped at the San Clemente checkpoint and our van was pulled over. The officer asked if we were all citizens and where we were going. My parents always told me to refuse to sign or say anything if I was ever asked about my immigration status. Fortunately in this case there were about eight of us in the van and everyone said yes, except I, but it seemed as if everyone had responded. I was really scared, and it's hard to explain the emotions that ran through me when the officer questioned us. One has to be in our shoes to be able to understand how frightened we immigrants, who live in the only country we know as home, are.

Imagine not seeing your family for eighteen years. I feel bad for myself, but my parents have not seen my grandparents since 1990. It's hard to for me to imagine not seeing my family for eighteen years. Years are passing by, and the situation becomes even more difficult as time passes because my grandparent's health was becoming a major issue. I once told my dad that

I'm willing to lose everything if we were to find out that my grandparents were going to die soon. My dad looked surprised when I told him that. I told him that we can always work hard and gain back what we lose, but no matter what we do, once a family member is gone, they're gone forever. My dad just smiled and said, you're right; that's not even a question; we have to go.

The Future

What I wished for was an immigration reform that's not just for students or people who have been here long enough; it's for everybody who deserves the chance to become legalized. Now that I'm at a CS University, it seems like my time to get legalized is running out. My major is International Business, which requires a mandatory study or internship abroad semester. I feel that it's extremely unfair to deny me my dreams and goals just because of my legal status, even though I'm willing to work as hard as it takes to be able to accomplish them. I currently have two part-time jobs. I work for dining services at the university (about fifteen to twenty hours/week) and I'm also a referee for (about ten to fifteen hours per week). Sometimes it's hard to make time for myself, the reason being that during the week sometimes I don't sleep or sleep only about two to three hours in order to finish my homework and study for tests. I'm a devoted Catholic, and I believe God would not put me in a situation I can't handle and he has a bright future planned for me. I believe there is a time and place for everything; my time has not come yet, but I really hope my time is near. I have accomplished so much despite my situation. I am very thankful for all my blessings and I have high hopes that President elect Barrack Obama will help my cause. The Dream Act would be exactly what I need at this point; I'm really excited for this upcoming year, hopefully there will be a long overdue immigration reform for everyone.

Summary

This chapter presented the lived experiences of eight college-aged students who reside in Southern California undocumented. Four of the participants attending community colleges and four attending the CSU or UC system. The students narrated their social dilemmas, struggles, and consequences of living undocumented. Chapter six presents the findings addressing the research question of the study.

Chapter 6

Findings

Chapter six provides a discussion of the research findings from semi-structured interviews, autobiographies, and follow-up personal meetings and responds to the research question of the study. The chapter is divided into three sections. Section one, provides and analyzes the themes emerging from the data collected and coded to address the research design. The second section, analyses the narratives and interviews from a legal, socio-logical and psychological perspective that seek to document explicit and implicit lived spaces of unauthorized Latino youth living in the United States. The third section provides a summary of the findings.

The guiding question for the study asked: What are the existing social-Psychological forces that shape the daily-lived experiences and negotiated spaces of unauthorized youth, in particular, those pursuing access to higher levels of education in the United States? To answer the main research question, three sub-questions were asked:

- What are the types of daily-lived situations that confront undocumented youths' sense of identity and belonging?
- What types of psychological trauma impacts how undocumented youth negotiate their daily-lived situations?
- How do Latino undocumented youth respond to the daily psychological trauma that they experience?

Case study methodology was selected as the best approach to capturing how unauthorized youth made sense of their lives and experiences, as well as their overall view of the world around them. Case studies produce more in-depth, comprehensive information by employing subjective information and participant observation to describe the context, or natural setting, of the concepts under consideration, as well as the interactions of the differ-ent concepts in the social context. Thus, case studies were used for a wide understanding of the entire lived conditions and situations experienced by undocumented youth in the study. The findings are presented for each of the three sub-questions as a way to answer the main question of the study.

Findings on Daily Lived Situations

The first sub-question of the study asked, *What are the types of daily-lived situations that confront undocumented youths' sense of identity and belonging?* To answer this question, eight themes were identified that described the types of daily lived situations confronting youths' sense of identity and belongingness. Using content analysis, Table 6.1 provides the themes derived from the study. For each theme a number of descriptors derived from the autobiography, interviews, and face-to-face dialogues were coded and allocated to the identified theme. Overall, eight (8) themes were identified.

For each theme some sample descriptors are provided to illustrate the type of issues mentioned by the eight participants. Table 6.1 also provides the number of descriptors found under each named theme. Overall 691 descriptors were identified, using triangulation of data. Appendix F provides one case study to illustrate the coding and documentation of descriptors.

	THEME	#	%
1.	Micro-Agressions	96	13.9
2.	Identity and Belongingness	94	13.6
3.	Trauma	127	18.4
4.	Resiliency, Adaptability, Pragmatism	87	12.6
5.	Membership	57	8.2
6.	Agency	30	4.3
7.	Family	67	9.7
8.	Structural Violence	192	19.2
	Total	691	99.9

Table 6.1 Frequencies

In terms of intensity, Structural violence with 192; Trauma had the highest descriptors with 127; Micro-aggressions with 96; Identity and Belongingness with 94; Resiliency, Adaptability, and Pragmatism with 87; Family with 67; Membership with 57; and Agency with 30. Following

Table 6.2, each theme is discussed and participant narrative statements used to illustrate focus of the theme.

Micro-aggressions

The micro-aggressions theme was derived from coded comments from the eight participants. Micro-aggression is defined as everyday interactions that send denigrating messages to a target group. Solorzano, Ceja, and Yosso (2000) document that the micro-aggressions are often subtle in nature and can be manifested in the verbal, nonverbal, visual, or behavioral realm and are often enacted automatically and unconsciously.

Micro-aggressions have been categorized by (Solorzano et al., 2000) in terms of (1) Micro-insults behavioral/verbal remarks or comments that convey rudeness, insensitivity, and demean a person's racial heritage or identity, (2) Micro-assault explicit racial derogations characterized primarily by a violent verbal or nonverbal attack meant to hurt the intended victim through name calling, avoidant behavior or purposeful discriminatory actions, (3) Micro-invalidations verbal comments or behaviors that exclude, negate, or nullify the psychological thoughts, feelings, or experiential reality of a person of color, and (4) Environmental micro-aggressions assaults, insults, and invalidations which are manifested on systemic and environmental levels (Solorzano et al., 2000).

THEME	INTERVIEW PROCESS	AUTO-BIO-GRAPHIES PROCESS	FACE-TO-FACE INTERVIEW PROCESS	TOTAL	EXAMPLE DESCRIPTORS
Micro-Aggressions	52	25	19	=96	• My friends make fun of my illegal status • People use offensive language about persons who are illegal • Constantly see the negative images the media portrays about undocumented people • Feeling less than human every time I need to prove who I am • Authorities remind me that I have no legal identity • When someone makes me feel less, I have no legal power or identity

(continued)

THEME	INTERVIEW PROCESS	AUTO-BIO-GRAPHIES PROCESS	FACE-TO-FACE INTERVIEW PROCESS	TOTAL	EXAMPLE DESCRIPTORS
Identity & Belongingness	35	28	31	=94	• I do not know if I belong • I have no place where I feel safe • I do not feel human living in trauma • My legal status has me under siege • I want to belong but with no legal identity • I have no future
Trauma	66	24	35	=127	• I could not stop shaking • I cried out of fear • I could not sleep thinking about my present status • I was scared to go out of my house • My mother cried, knowing we had no legal status
Resiliency, Adaptability and Pragmatism	19	45	23	=87	• Marriage with a legal citizen • I will continue education despite my legal limitations • I will work hard to achieve legal status • A fake Social Security card is my only survival • Hope is my constant companion • Assimilate to socially blend • Wake-up to a new day • Finding supporting spaces • Understanding the habits of racism • Knowing my rights as a human being
Membership	8	33	16	=57	• We are not American • I was not born in the U.S. • Can't be part of a group • Not allowed to enter • I feel like a shadow • I have no ID

THEME	INTERVIEW PROCESS	AUTO-BIO-GRAPHIES PROCESS	FACE-TO-FACE INTERVIEW PROCESS	TOTAL	EXAMPLE DESCRIPTORS
Agency	8	14	8	=30	• Hope to make changes once I become legal • I will help others to prevent them feeling Helpless • Will work to change immigration policy • I want to teach social justice • I want to make a difference
Family	19	37	11	=67	• Sacrifices to improve • Commitment to each other • Always provided food • Faith in my future • Safety was always a concern for my family
Structural Violence	23	34	76	=133	• Persecuted • National threat • Racial profile • Denied human rights • No medical attention • Marginalized • Racist messages • Labeled outlaw • Treated differently

Table 6.2 Content Analysis of Unauthorized Student Voices by Theme, Data Collection Process, and Number of Descriptors Mentioned

In analyzing the data of daily-lived situations confronting undocumented youth, micro-aggression was a consistent theme. In the vast majority of the cases, micro-insult violence was present in the form of insensitivity to legal status or demeaning racial comments that caused emotional discomfort.

During the follow up interview with **Linda,** she commented on the constant exposure to insensitive comments at work and in her social circles.

All my life I have heard people use words that caused me to feel uncomfortable and have reduced my humanity. At work, for example, when I worked at a restaurant or even with the family members of my ex-boyfriend, I would hear people use the word **wetback** *when they talked about Mexican immigrants. I felt anger but also helpless, unable to say anything. Even when I knew that the people were not racist, it still hurt me.*

It is important to note that insults, behavioral, verbal, and nonverbal remarks considered emotionally painful by the participants of the study were often made by other Mexican-origin children or even people within the close social circles of the participants. **Rocky** feels his friends are not fully conscious of what they are saying or doing in terms of micro-insults.

> *Whenever my friends talk about going out, they will often joke about going to places where they know I cannot go. Or they will say things like, "It's your turn to drive," when they know I do not have a license. They do not know how much I wish I could get a driver's license and that I would be happy to always be the driver wherever we go. But I can't. I can't get a license.*

While the role of media can be analyzed under the concept of structural violence, the impact of the consistency and subtlety of media messages are noted here as part of micro-assaults. For most participants in the study, the communications media plays a major role in the construction of negative images of unauthorized immigrants in general and of unauthorized youth in particular. Participants noted news media and stereotypes in the television and film industry as spreading negative stereotypes of the undocumented population. **Maria** notes in the follow up interview the dangers she sees in negative images.

> *Every time I see the news the only thing that is reported on are the bad things done by immigrants, especially illegal Mexican immigrants. There are no stories of the accomplishments. There are no stories of the good hard working people. This is dangerous, especially in this type of economy. Not hearing good things and only being exposed to bad ones little by little creates fear and anger and stereotypes in people.*

Experiencing micro-aggression on a daily basis was a consistent subject in all narratives and interviews and is connected to the coded theme of identity and belonging.

Identity and Belonging

In analyzing the data of daily-lived situations confronting undocumented youth, a sense of identity and belonging was also coded as a consistent theme. The concept of belonging is a powerful lens for which to examine immigrant integration in modern times (Mulgan, 2008). For French philosopher Albert Camus, one of the most painful questions asked is "Where is home?" It is an inquiry that has less to do with geography and more to do with identity, space, and membership.

The eight case studies of undocumented youth in the United States constantly reminded us how they are continuously confronted with a barrage of obstacles that are a consistent reminder of their legal status and virtual incarceration. The narratives reveal an array of daily-lived situations confronting the undocumented youths' sense of identity and belonging.

If we take into account the basic human need to "belong," or the seeking of membership, the true impact of living always on the periphery or in shadows of society is revealed. All narratives included segments were the youths' sense of identity and belonging is questioned. Reflections of the narratives reveal and highlight the issue of belonging.

From very early in her life, **Brenda** was confronted with the reality of her legal status in the United States. Moreover, throughout her young life, she has felt like she did not belong and, thus, she had no rights. These feelings are largely a product of her illegal status and the lack of rights and opportunities that come with her lived reality. Brenda commented on a confrontation with an employer that cemented her view that she had no rights since she was not legally in the country.

> *I decided to confront the owner one day and ask him why I was not getting paid all the hours that I had worked. He replied, "You have no right to tell me what to pay you because you are an illegal immigrant, and if you don't like it I can fire you." I felt so terrible that day and I went home crying, but I did not let my mom see me or know why I was crying.*

Maria tells of similar emotions with identity and belonging in a traumatizing event that involved the San Diego police department. Ironically Maria's childhood had been largely unaffected by her legal status. While she negotiated her legal status throughout her life, it was this episode with police that made her confront the reality of regulated social policy.

> *I had never been treated like a criminal. This incident was a huge wakeup call for me. Yes, I did come to this country illegally, but I was never treated like I was. For the first time in my life, I felt what it's like to be seen different in someone else's eyes because I was not born in the United States.*

For **Rocky**, the issues of identity and belonging have not always been directly associated with confrontation with law enforcement in regulated legal spaces and policy. Rocky comments on the social impact of credentials or the lack of them as they pertain to a social context. One year, while back home for the summer as a college student he was denied membership to a gym, an episode that would mark him.

> *Not having a California I.D. has really had an impact in my life. My friends and I were going to work out at a gym during the summer break, but in order for me to be able to start a gym membership, I needed a California I.D. Unfortunately, as an undocumented person, I could not get one and I couldn't join the gym. My friends felt really bad. I decided to work out at home, but it really frustrated me that I wasn't able to bond with my high school friends and share our college stories.*

It is perhaps in the social context that young college-aged unauthorized youth experience much of the pressure regarding social practice and legal status. These tensions go far beyond a membership in a gym. This is especially true in Southern California and other border cities were college students travel south of the border for entertainment. There exists great strain on unauthorized youth, especially in the social context, to not be discriminated or marginalized by peers for not being legal. They are careful to whom they reveal their legal status and how they navigate their implicit and explicit social space.

In the case of **Chuy,** he reflects on the social pressures that exist in college and the need to be accepted, to belong.

> *Being in college was a privilege, yet the social atmosphere was limited for people like me. Usually by now people are of legal age, and, since we are so close to the border, people want to go to TJ, a place to go clubbing and be able to drink legally. The friends I did make at State in my freshman year would always call my cell and tell me to go with them to TJ. I would always tell them some story like, "No, I can't, I'm babysitting," or "No I can't, I have to go to work tomorrow at five in the morning." They would always keep asking, so I came up with a story to tell them why I would not go back. I told them I was once in TJ when I was sixteen years old with my friends and we were just walking around just to see what things we wanted to buy, when some guys came to us and beat the living shit out of us. My friend being a tough guy got up and talked smack back to them until they pull a gun and shot him in front of my face. Coming back to San Diego I told his mom, and, well it was an experience that still haunts me. THAT'S WHY I DON'T GO TO TJ. After I told them this little lie, they would never try to persuade me to go to TJ with them again.*

The theme of identity and belonging was a dominant theme in all eight case studies and present in every narrative and interview. A comparable theme that was consistently mentioned was that of trauma. Trauma was felt as a feeling of rejection and the pressures to be accepted. The experience of trauma is the third dominant theme of the findings.

Trauma

Trauma here is defined from a psychological perspective as the feeling of fear, stress, depression, exclusion, and apprehension as a result of having unauthorized status. Based on the coded responses of the eight participants, there exist several types of psychological trauma impacting how undocumented youth negotiate their daily-lived situations.

One of these types of trauma involves the recollection of distressing events in one's life. Trauma is a psychological distressing experience outside the range of common human experience. It can occur as the result of months or years of abuse or neglect, or in the wake of a single overwhelming event. Trauma often involves a sense of fear, terror, and helplessness in the face of real or perceived threat to one's or a loved one's well-being (Perry, 2006).

In the case of **Chuy**, apprehension, deportation, and family separation by immigration authorities generated conditions of trauma or posttraumatic disorder syndrome. Chuy recalls a childhood memory when he and his mother were detained and deported. It was a moment he says he will never forget and has caused emotional anxiety.

> *After we got caught, they made us go into the migra car, which fit about seven of us. I thought to myself, we were now on our way back to Mexico. The migra that caught us took us to a place where there was a bus, and transported us back to where we were going to get processed. I still remember my mom being upset that we got caught, and the money the coyote had taken which she had saved up for very long time. I was crying on the bus and I also saw more people mostly Mexican looking who had also been caught. My mom told me to cheer up and told me that everything was going to be okay. I didn't know what her plan was, but I believed her and wiped my tears away and fell asleep in her lap.*

Arrest, deportation, and separation of the family by immigration authorities can produce tremendous anxiety. Trauma is an experience that induces an abnormally intense and prolonged stress response. It overwhelms a person's ability to cope. Common effects or conditions that may occur include physical, emotional, and cognitive responses such as sleep disturbances, depression, anxiety, distraction, avoidance, and hyper-vigilance (Capps et al., 2007; Perry, 2006).

Norma recalls the emotional depression she suffered when her mother was taken to a women's prison. Norma's grades in college dropped, as did her overall health when ICE arrested her mother. She recounts.

In January of 2007 my mother received a letter from the district attorney's office stating she was being charged with three felonies because she used false documentation to obtain a job. As usual, she took it as casual things but I knew that the problem wouldn't go away that easily. She was set to attend court a month later and there she was told that she could be booked and perhaps taken to the women's detention facility in Santee California known as Las Colinas. When she did so she was detained by ICE and held for about two days before my family was able to bail her out. Thereafter a series of never-ending court appearances proceeded. We had to get a lawyer, who ended up taking advantage of us. He did nothing to help my mother instead his actions landed her in jail one more time, but this time for nearly a month in late August of this year. It has been a horrible nightmare.

The fear of apprehension and deportation is such that the news media reports revealed the fear of immigration raids that has sent families into hiding in the basement or closets of their homes for days and sometimes weeks at a time (Capps et al., 2007).

Linda remembers a similar situation in her childhood, which could have ended in a tragedy and loss of life and which haunts her to this day.

The summers were extremely hot and my brothers and I were not allowed to play outside. My parents were afraid that someone would realize that we lived there and deport us. At one point there was a gas leak in the garage and my mother, brothers, and I almost died. My dad got home from work just in time.

The traumatic events these youth experience in many ways provide the college-age participants the strength to survive in the larger context of their lived spaces. While the lived events and experiences in their daily lives are painful and disturbing, they remain standing and, moreover, in their own way, thriving despite their legal obstacles. This is due in part to their ability to adapt and be pragmatic and resilient, an additional coded theme that was found across the eight participants of the study.

Resiliency, Adaptability, and Pragmatism

Latino undocumented youth often respond to the daily psychological trauma that they experience with pragmatism, incredible adaptability, and resiliency. Confronted with legal, financial, and other social obstacles, they are consistently constructing ways to create support systems and find avenues and spaces where not only can they exist, but thrive. Diego highlights the importance of community support and the desire to pursue an education despite his legal challenges. **Diego** recalls the importance of adapting to information and opportunity when information on college was not part of the agenda of his high school counselors.

> *Thanks to my friend Roberto whom I met in the church's youth group, I found out about the Assembly Bill 540 (AB540), which made tuition affordable for immigrant students. He was enrolled in college under the same bill, so he helped me fill out the paperwork and enroll in a community college. Thanks to his help, I stayed here to study and did not go to Mexico. I still can't understand why my high school counselors never told me about this; they knew my situation and still never told me I could continue my education in the United States.*

Employment is often a very challenging activity, and yet many of the participants are currently employed. Methods to obtain employment are many, but often in the context of exploitation, as was the case with Norma's mother who was incarcerated for using unauthorized documents to get a job. Still, the desire to work and earn money is such that the limits are tested. Linda's experiences serve as another example. Even now, she still works with the same (expired temporary visa) card as she did when she got her first job at Disneyland.

Finding a way to find employment is highly problematic, and the risk-taking emotionally stressful, as in the case of **Linda.**

> *Someone gave me the idea of erasing the "NOT VALID FOR EMPLOYMENT" of my real government card, I did that and it worked! I worked for Mickey Mouse at the happiest place on earth for five years. I worked there my senior year of high school and all the way through community college. I am still employed using that same card.*

Still, even as resilient as the unauthorized youth are, the pressures they face are real and traumatizing. The limitations are paramount even in choosing an academic major.

Moreover, the avenues sought to escape their reality of being unauthorized often can be themselves traumatic. Consider the following. All female participants saw marriage as a means of obtaining legal status. Marriage, it should be noted, is a legitimate path to legal status. Arranged marriages, however, while perceived, as examples of resiliency and adaptability, can also be indicators or inducers of further trauma. **Maria** highlights this point when she comments on her ordeal with San Diego Police.

> *I have never really thought about getting married to get my citizenship, but this incident really traumatized me. It has been something that I have been thinking about doing because I really want to be legal. I want to be able to drive a car with a license, and be insured. I have not been able to get behind the wheel again because of my fear of getting pulled over and/ or getting the car impounded and/or getting a ticket. I am also stressed out about choosing a major and a career because of my current situation. I want to be able to choose a career that I really want and not because I think I will be able to cheat the system.*

While resiliency, adaptability, and pragmatism can be perceived as positive characteristics, the researcher suggests these behaviors also can be perilous and hurtful to the unauthorized college-age population. In their impetus to achieve their goals, they run the risk of their legal status being revealed. Moreover, they can become victims of financial and physical abuse.

The ability to adapt to one's environment and personal challenges also comes at the price of exclusion—not having the legal papers to have access to public areas where legal identity is required. This leads us to the coded theme of membership.

Membership

The subject of membership is best analyzed within the frame of exclusion and inclusion. Content analysis of unauthorized student voices offers descriptors of membership that stress feelings of segregation, omission, prohibition, and even invisibility. Comments such as "We are not Americans" and remarks on exclusion from places or events due to the lack of valid forms of identification are common in the narratives. In a follow up interview with **Maria**, she added to her feelings expressed in her autobiography regarding her ordeal with the police.

> *For the first time in my life, I felt what it's like to be seen as different in someone else's eyes because I was not born in the United States. I was not an American. If I had been born in this country, I would have been treated differently or at least I would have the right to defend myself. But I am not, so I am seen as not being a member of this society and without rights even to be treated as a human.*

Maria's problems were not having a driver's license or any form of I.D other than her school Identification. In a society where a driver's license is equated with establishing identity, to be denied one is analogous to denying membership. The impact of not having an identification document varies from the denial of gym membership to being locked out of a fundamental component of the American economy, such as credit. **Rocky** commented on the exclusion from places.

> *Not having a driver's license or any accepted valid form of identification is really hard. I cannot enter places were an I.D. is required. For example night clubs are out of the question. Without a valid I.D., you are not allowed to enter. Many times my fraternity has invited me to national meetings, but I cannot go because I do not have an I.D. We cannot fly anywhere because of the lack of proper identification.*

Many of the participants expressed that they felt like they were living in the shadows. Such feelings are produced by a society that dehumanizes a group of people often reducing them to statistics and stereotypes without addressing questions of economic vortexes, immigration policy, and incorporation into American society. **Diego** begins his autobiography with this reflection.

> *Like me, there are many others who have lost their voices and whose stories haven't been told. I am one of many, living in the shadows of American society. A foreigner caught in a system where "barriers" are built day after day, barriers which seem to be created to prevent success, built to keep us from reaching our goals and unleashing our potential.*

The feelings of rejections and denial of membership while debilitating also inspire the participants to be active agents of change. Their willingness to participate in this study is but one example of agency.

Agency

Agency was another theme that consistently appears in the narratives and expressed in the interviews. The college-age participants expressed wanting to be agents of change and not just passive victims or observers. The fact that they took part in this study is evidence of being active agents in sharing their lived situations. Most participants look forward to a time not only when the law will change and give them legal status in the United States, but also to have the chance to help others. **Diego** passionately describes these feelings.

Just like me there are many others who have suffered injustice, rejection, worked hard day and night to achieve their goals, and no matter how big the barriers are, they still have the courage to fight and climb. The time is now, to have open ears, to see through our eyes, walk in our shoes and feel what we feel. It hasn't been easy for my family and I and I hope people make conscious of the difficulties illegal immigrants face. I believe people will listen, understand and react. I have faith, and in faith there is always hope.

It is provoking for unauthorized college-aged youth to see American citizens or those with legal residence with rights and opportunities and not take advantages of them. **Chuy** reflects on his choices as a young man.

There are limited things that a teenager can do without having papers in this country. Thankfully one of them is going to school and getting good grades, and to hope for the best, the best meaning going to college. Others choose alternative options and one of them is dropping out of school, and getting a job, and another one is joining gangs. I decided to do none of the last two and since I was a smart kid. I knew that if I was to have a future in this country, it was going to be through my education, not through being a criminal or just working to get money right away. I got good grades and was a good athlete as well.

The desire to be active members in society and in changing immigration policy is matched only by their desire to be creators, contributors, and successful Americans.

Linda like other participants in this study sees herself actively assisting others when her legal status changes.

Although I would like to visit Mexico soon, I am thankful that I grew up here. I am thankful for all the opportunities that Los Estados Unidos has given me. I hope that in the future I will be able to help other immigrants grasp the opportunities that lay before them. These opportunities may not seem so apparent at first and are not that easy to grasp, but they are there. We can all be successful.

While regretting the inability to visit the homeland of their parents, the eight participants named family as another salient theme.

Family

Family is without failure addressed in all eight accounts. All participants cite the sacrifice and relentless support of their families. Participants appreciate all aspects of their family life from their parents leaving their homeland, crossing the border unauthorized, to seek work. This is something their parents have done for them to have a better life. Like many of the participants, in fact, like most immigrants, **Linda** remembers the day she left the place where she was born and the loved ones left behind. The separation of families is one of the human costs and traumatic consequences of immigration policy.

> *I was excited, but I remember seeing tears run down my mother's face when she said goodbye to her mother, my grandmother. At the time, I didn't know that I would no longer see my sweet "mami chui," that's what I called my grandma. I also didn't know that I would never see the vibrant city that I used to call home. Well, at least I haven't yet.*

The crossing of the border is a like a rite of passage for most immigrants. The experience of crossing the border unauthorized is a traumatic and dangerous activity. The perils that loom and the emotional experience of families crossing the border create a special and lasting memory—a negative emotional experience. Many of the participants like **Norma** recall the crossing.

> *My uncle Gabriel carried me the entire time and my uncle Angel was carrying my brother. My mother would help my aunt Laura because of her pregnant condition. We traveled through the desert for an entire day. I remember being very tired, thirsty, and most of all scared because there were times when everyone would run or hide. My mother remembers me questioning everything we did. I could not understand the reasons for or what we were doing that.*

Our parents, certainly those who crossed the southern border from Mexico, always spoke of "*una vida mejor*" or a better life for their loved ones, their children. Being legally or illegally in the United States never stopped parents from wanting the best for their children and wanting them to feel safe and included. Rocky highlights these parental feelings when he recalls how his parents encouraged him, despite the legal limitations in the United States.

> *I was too young to understand the legal system, but my parents would always tell me to get good grades, go to college, and nothing was ever going to stop me from doing what I wanted to do. I joined the junior varsity football team at my high school, and it seemed from that point on everything I did had to be different. All my teammates had medical insurance, and they would easily go to their private doctor to get physicals to be able*

to play. I remember how my mother and I had to shop around to get the cheapest price for a physical since I wasn't able to get medical insurance.

Structural Violence

Structural violence is generally defined as institutionalized social injustices. It is set apart from direct violence and its brutality, but its impact can be equally physically damaging, even deadly. Structural violence is the product of unjust legal systems and social policy, as well as ingrained beliefs, that deny certain members of the populace access to the available social, economic, political, or even cultural opportunities. Much of the damage from structural violence comes from longstanding structural inequities which are accepted as norm by the larger society. It becomes embedded in ubiquitous social structures (Lemert, 2003).

Structural violence produces damage by the rigidity and inflexibility of the sociopolitical, as well as economic, organization toward the target population. Membership, gender, race, class, as well as religion, have historically been the basis for social injustice and perpetuated structural violence. Segregation, second class citizenship, chronic oppression, as well as exile, have often been the instrumentation of structural violence (Kohler and Alcock, 1976).

With the recent outbreak in 2009 of the HINI Flu Virus, some of the subjects of the study expressed their concerns over access to health care. For most of their lives they have feared that access to medical attention may lead to exposure of their legal status. Part of their fear arises from laws, such as California's Proposition 187 in 1994 which, while found to be unconstitutional, left many in fear. During her last interview **Norma** reflected on issues of health care.

> *I don't recall going to the doctor when I was a child; my mother was always afraid that we could get caught or that it would be used against us when we tried to become legal. When we got sick, friends of my father would bring us medicine from Tijuana, like penicillin, for example.*

In its broader definition, structural violence includes harm to the dignity and freedom of individuals. Of particular interest for the researcher was the association by a few scholars between structural violence and labeling theory. For such scholars, labeling is an example of the structural violence as it relates to the language of the social system. A person's self can be stigmatized or tainted by public labeling. It is structurally violent because it defines someone's identity with respect to another's rules and perceptions of behavior (Lemert, 2003).

The person labeled is often not part of the establishing definition and simply has the label applied to him/her with no particular regard for his/her situations. The labels of "illegal" or even "AB540 Student" transmit a certain stigma in American society. Not being "within the law" or being "foreign," as well as access, are easily made associations by the general public. The Labeling harms the person through the denial to his/her own existence, and discredits one of any possible contributions to American society. Moreover, the impact on self-esteem can be disastrous.

Among the participants in this study the researcher finds labeling as part of structural violence to be a powerful stigma in most of the cases. In some cases, in fact, labeling has a paralyzing effect. **Brenda** commented on labeling.

> *Everywere I go, anything I see, and everything I do is controlled by being illegally in the United States. On television, in the streets, and even in my dreams that word* illegal *terrorizes me. Even in class, in school with my counselor, the word comes out as if there was something wrong with me, as if I was guilty, always guilty, of something I had no control over.*

The same feelings of oppression from labeling are expressed by **Linda**, but with a certain taste of fortitude, as she stated in her last interview her feelings on language.

> *People at work or at school use the word* illegal *or even* wetback, *and I just wish I could respond and say I am one of those people you claim are taking your jobs or abusing the system. These are the same people who I know do not take advantage of what they have, and yet they bitch that some else might. They could get financial aid and go to school, but they do not. I cannot stand it, but I cannot say anything either. Maybe one day I will, but for now I just have to ignore it and shut up.*

While the eight themes have common narratives, it is evident that the participants respond differently to the lived situations in which those themes are expressed. In the face-to-face interviews, each individual responded differently to the social and legal spaces they have confronted. Nevertheless, each of the eight themes described the daily lived experiences and tensions of being unauthorized and living in the margins of society.

Finding Types of Psychological Trauma and Responses

In the next section, the findings to sub-question two and three of the study are presented. These questions asked:

- What types of psychological trauma impacts how undocumented youth negotiate their daily-lived situations?
- How do Latino undocumented youth respond to the daily psychological trauma that they experience?

The findings of the study suggest that the psychological stress experienced by undocumented youth builds up as they enter high school and college age. The narratives and voices of the eight participants indicate that high school marked a critical time in their lives. High school became the years of harsh truth that they are living in the United States unauthorized and restrained by their legal status. Access to higher education for undocumented students is a highly contested issue. Federal and state governments, while considering the issue of supporting successful undocumented high school students, is non-existent when it comes to policy that invests in youth who have lived in the United States since their elementary school year and in their future.

The findings to two the sub-questions of the study are presented under two dimensions. The first consists of explicit and implicit modes of behavior—behaviors that are seen by others who interact with the individual (explicit) and behaviors that are not seen by others (implicit). The second dimension consists of the legal status of the individual or the unauthorized status of interacting and living in the United States. The conceptual framework in chapter one is reintroduced (Figure 6.1) to guide the reader.

The first dimension centers on the psychological dynamics faced by the unauthorized students. The second dimension is a legal measurement that is expressed from a legal continuum—at one end are unauthorized and unregulated social policies where the individual is able to negotiate his/her lived space by interacting in an environment with which s/he is very familiar. At the other end are unauthorized and regulated social policies where the individual interacts in public spaces while running the risk of being apprehended for not having the legal documentation.

The socio-psychological lived space dimension is expressed as explicit lived space and implicit lived space. The explicit lived space is what the individual is willing to share or is known to him/her and others. The implicit lived space is what the individual is not willing to share with others that s/he interacts with.

The four-quadrant framework suggests a way for measuring variance in the social integration of the unauthorized person in his/her community.

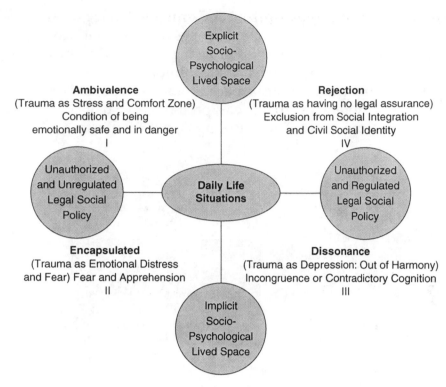

Figure 6.1 Conceptual framework for understanding the socio-psychology of lived spaces and regulated social policy in residing in the United States

Moreover, it reveals the types of psychological trauma experienced by the person, such as stress and depression, emotional distress, and having no sense of legal assurance of his/her lived status from day to day. In the case of undocumented youth/college-age students living in the U.S., the findings lead us to the analysis of the four quadrants under the headings of ambivalence, encapsulation, dissonance, and rejection.

Ambivalence

Ambivalence best describes the first quadrant. Ambivalence is a state of living in a part of the community where he/she feels familiar and has a high degree of awareness of civic behavior while understanding his/her legal status and while interacting in low-risk social activities that are part of the daily social dynamics of the community. S/he, while experiencing a sense of "zone of comfort" in the community, nevertheless has the constant worry or trauma of not being "legal" and living under stress. Involvement in such activities include going to local stores, church functions, or family gatherings in a park that are enjoyed, but not without the fear of legal ramifications.

In the first quadrant (unauthorized and unregulated legal social policy and explicit lived space), the study findings suggest that the undocumented youth do experience ambivalence. The eight college-age youth experienced psychological trauma by expressing a constant emotional stress and danger that forces them to know what physical space is perceived as safe or what comfort zone s/he is able to interact with the least problems—usually the surroundings of his/her place of residence. The following Figure 6.2 illustrates Quadrant I:

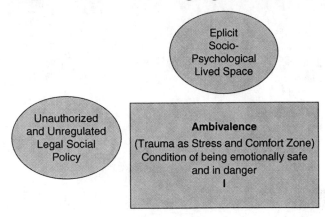

Figure 6.2 Ambivalence

All eight participants in the study navigate this quadrant, with Linda and Brenda navigating this quadrant with more frequency in their narratives. Linda comments how going home to see her family, while a joyful occasion, also generated personal tensions. Brenda expressed a sense of feeling comfortable living in a largely Mexican barrio in San Diego, California. Everyone around her knows her status. In fact, a significant number of people who live in that area have her same legal status. Nevertheless, she is aware of the perils that loom every time she and her mother step into the streets.

Overall, Linda was fairly confident about not being apprehended by authorities, given that as an adult she had not experienced any close encounters with immigration agencies. She, in fact, like many of the other participants, regularly traveled across immigration checkpoints, crossings that generate a feeling of great apprehension and discomfort. For Linda such moments created a sense of abnormality and physical and emotional stress.

> *When I go home to Los Angeles to see my family, I have to cross the checkpoint at San Clemente. I remember the first time. I was eager and excited to go home, but I had to cross the immigration checkpoint. I used to think that the immigration had supersensitive hearing devises to listen to what people were saying or listening to. I would always stop playing*

my Mexican music like Vicente Fernandez and play English music just in case. I know it is silly, but that is the kind of stuff that comes to your mind.

In the case of Brenda, she expressed the constant stress of worrying about her mother and herself being apprehended by some legal authorities.

My mom works every day cleaning houses. She has to go on the bus or the trolley every day, and sometimes I get scared because the other day the police got onboard the trolley and were asking people for their immigration papers. Thank God she was not on that train yet. However, one day that could happen to her. I hope not. I get scared. I am scared one day she might get detained and I'll never see her again.

Encapsulation

Under the second quadrant (unauthorized and unregulated legal social policy and implicit socio-psychological lived space) the undocumented youth experiences are best described as encapsulation. This state of encapsulation is defined as trauma experience by emotional distress and fear. Encapsulation is illustrated as a state of constant fear and apprehension known only to him/her or their intimate others.

In the study, the eight college-age youth expressed being constantly aware that s/he must always be on the lookout and needing to negotiate the lived spaces that offer him/her a sense of control. Teachers, peers, and fellow students are unaware of his/her legal status in the implicit lived space. Therefore, a school fieldtrip designed to be educational and fun, can elicit feelings of fear and apprehension in the unauthorized students, given that legal and disclosure barriers may be present. The following Figure 6.3 illustrates Quadrant II:

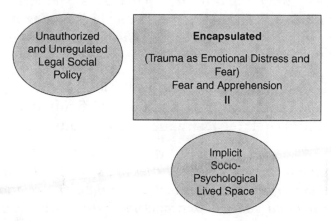

Figure 6.3 Encapsulated

Rocky illustrates such fear and apprehension through his comments about an experience he had as a member of a fraternity in a southern California university while on a trip.

> One of the closest experiences I've ever had to possibly being deported was in April 2007. My fraternity had a nationwide event at Colorado State University, and we rented a van to road trip over there. We were stopped at the San Clemente checkpoint and our van was pulled over. The officer asked if we were all citizens and where we were going. My parents always told me to refuse to sign or say anything if I was ever asked about my immigration status. Fortunately in this case there were about eight of us in the van and everyone said yes, except me, but it seemed as if everyone had responded. I was really scared, and it's hard to explain the emotions that ran through me when the officer questioned us. One has to be in our shoes to be able to understand how frightened we immigrants, who live in the only country we know as home, are.

The pressure experienced by college-age unauthorized youth to navigate the implicit space is personally overwhelming. Who can be trusted with such delicate information is a gut-wrenching question. Especially as one seeks an avenue of social support. Chuy discusses why he would tell lies to his peers when they insisted he cross the border and socialize with them in Tijuana, Mexico.

> I know this made-up story is bad in a sense of why make up that story instead of telling them the truth. The truth is that I didn't trust them. It's hard for me to come out to someone and tell them, yeah, I am an illegal so I can't go to Mexico. Being an illegal, I have to watch my moves; I can't go around telling people or friends that I just met that I'm an alien because when it comes down to it, maybe one of them doesn't like me or feels that his girl is hot for me, so he calls the migra on me and my whole journey that I've made to college is done.

In their narratives Linda, Maria, and Pedro look at the impact of their legal status on dating. They all shared that it was difficult to inform the people they have dated about their legal situation. Linda commented on her dating experiences.

> I have dated guys who have repeatedly asked me to go with them dancing to clubs in Tijuana or even travel abroad when the relationship has matured. But how do you tell someone you cannot go because you are illegal? So I make up excuses or tell them that we will go next month. On

one occasion, I was going shopping with someone and before I noticed we were close to the border. I panicked and I wanted to yell, "Stop." Luckily we got off on the last U.S. exit.

Dissonance

Under Quadrant III (unauthorized and regulated legal social policy and implicit lived space), the undocumented youth experiences are best described as dissonance. This state of dissonance is defined as trauma experienced in the form of depression and the feeling of being out of harmony with one's surroundings. Dissonance, thus, is a state of living in trauma and out of harmony within the community and within the self. The inability to share the legal status with others creates an inner conflict, a feeling of helplessness, incongruence or contradictory cognition, and often depression. A simple college night out with friends to local establishments that require a driver's license for identification becomes an emotional test for unauthorized individuals. The following Figure 6.4 illustrates Quadrant III:

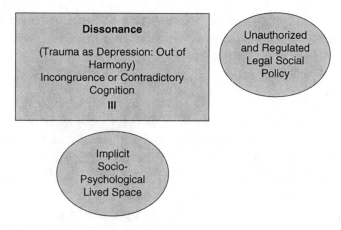

Figure 6.4 Dissonance

The narratives and face-to-face interviews with the eight participants suggest that there are clear and powerful emotions behind each person's lived experiences. The feeling of being incarcerated and feeling a sense of hopelessness is a powerful emotion described by each participant. In the case of Rocky, he shared his emotions about not being able to obtain a drivers license.

It's really depressing to live life knowing I can't get a driver's license to drive back home and visit my family, or take a girl out on a date without her having to drive, go to any club I want without the risk of getting denied entry, consider getting a loan when I have no money to eat nor-mally at times, and be able to apply for a good job/internship regardless of the requirements.

Rocky also expressed a feeling of dissonance, not knowing what to do to remedy his situation, when he recently applied for an internship required under his International Business major. After making the first cut, he was called back for a second interview, where he would meet the president of a business in the San Diego region as a second tier process for the internship. He was thrilled; being a business major, he knew this internship was important and something he wanted to do since he was in college. Unfortunately he was not given a chance to even start the second interview because he revealed he did not have a driver's license or a car, which was a mandatory requirement to qualify for the internship.

I must admit I cried when I got home from the frustration and disappoint-ment when I got denied acceptance due to something I couldn't control. My interviewer mentioned that only about 5 percent of students advance to the second interview with the president.

It is difficult, if not impossible, to measure the emotional negative impact of having so much "ganas"/desire to work and succeed and find walls and obstacles all around you. In another case, Brenda recollects the first time she wanted to work and realized that legally she could not.

I was sixteen years old now and I was desperate to find a job. I went to look for one, but I soon received bad news from my mom. After I had told my mom that I wanted to work, she told me that I was not going to have luck finding a job. I couldn't get a job because I am undocumented and don't have a social security number which is required for anyone to work legally in this country. I remember feeling really down that day because I felt as though all my dreams were thrown out the window.

For the eight unauthorized youth in the study, all expressed that they periodically felt in a state of dissonance of wanting to improve themselves and often feeling rejected, an exhausting emotional sense of trauma.

Rejection

Under Quadrant IV (unauthorized and regulated legal social policy and ex-plicit lived space), the undocumented youth experiences can be best de-scribed as rejection. This state of rejection is defined as trauma experienced through social exclusion. Rejection is also a state of living outside of the community where he/she feels excluded from civic participation. In this quadrant, the individual suffers the trauma of having no legal assurance of being treated fairly, and within the law and feeling excluded from social being integrated into the community or having a civil social identity. All eight unauthorized participants expressed this sense of exclusion—living in the community and not being part of its civic life. Not being able to take part in the political process by exerting their voices through the voting process serves as an example of such exclusion from social and civic integration. The following Figure 6.5 illustrates Quadrant IV:

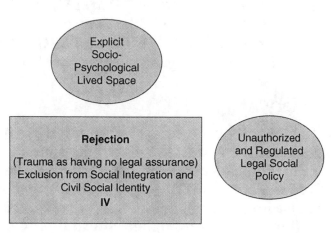

Figure 6.5 Rejection

While most participants in the study have been situated in this space Brenda expressed a strong sense of feeling rejection.

> *I saw many of my co-workers get spit on and harassed by the drunken customers. I was so young and saw very wrong things that people will do to each other. But I couldn't say anything, because again I did not have the right to talk. I was undocumented and I had to always remain self-conscious about that.*

In the case of Chuy and Pedro, like other participants, they describe the challenges faced by unauthorized college-age students with tuition costs and denial of financial assistance. This directly makes you different because you are not even considered for financial assistance or consideration of possible future employment opportunities. For Chuy, finding work to earn money and paying for school expenses is a constant struggle.

> *Money was scarce, but to an illegal immigrant money was even harder to get. We don't have the right to work in this country nor do we get any*

government help, to provide for people like me, who desire to keep going and continue their education. We are left out from the rest of the students who wish to go to college, and since we can't work we have to find other means to pay for our education.

Pedro, motivated to study and go to college, soon realized in his second year of high school that his life situation was going to be very difficult.

It was my junior year when I finally thought about what college I wanted to attend and how I was going to pay for it. That's when it hit me that I didn't have any money and I wasn't going to be able to apply for FASFA or other financial aid because they required a social security number, which I didn't have. It frustrated me to think that I tried so hard, got 4.0 GPA for three years and I wasn't even going to be able to go to college because I couldn't afford it.

Reflective Summary

The conceptual framework of the study incorporating two dimensions of lived spaces serves to reflect on the struggles of the eight unauthorized participants, specifically the types of trauma they feel on a daily basis as they negotiate their lived environment. The eight participants remind us of past injustices and the disastrous immigration policy that is painfully evident in American schools (kindergarten to higher education). In schools undocumented students live in constant fear of their status of being disclosed, and, despite their educational success, their dreams and professional objectives are currently futureless. The narratives of the eight participants of the study also remind us of what is going on in American colleges and universities where the criminalization and virtual internment of undocumented youth are painfully evident.

Because of their illegal status, these youth have lived their lives bounded by socio-psychological forces that shape their daily-lived experiences and have been forced to consistently negotiate social and legal spaces. The legal and political conditions have catapulted these youth into an arena where they have to negotiate the tensions produced by their official immigration status as unauthorized individuals.

The complexity of their world is painfully clear in the narratives. Their world is demarcated by incompatible legal parameters, some denoting regulated social policy, while others are evidently creating spaces were unregulated social policy exist. As such, unauthorized youth have to consistently alter and adapt their lived situations. One moment they may be gifted college students in an unregulated legal space (college campus) and the very next they are committing a federal crime by being in the United States unauthorized (outside of college campus).

The narratives served as a window into the lives of the unauthorized student population in the United States.

The next chapter will reflect on the findings of the study with regard to the main research question, reflect on the implications of the study, and provide recommendations for further research.

The narrative analysis and the data rendered responded to the research question of the study. Data analysis of the case studies, allowed the researcher to identify consistent themes from all the information collected, which included interviews, autobiographies, and follow-up face-to-face meetings with the participants. In analyzing the data, themes emerged that address the research design. These themes included Micro-aggressions, Identity and Belonging, Trauma, Resiliency-Adaptability-Pragmatism, Membership, Agency, Family, Membership, and Structural Violence. What follows is a reflection of the selected themes as they appear in the narratives. In responding to the research question, the data first points to a common thread of themes in lived spaces of the unauthorized college-age student population, such as identity, membership, trauma, adaptability, pragmatism, agency, and family.

Second, the research indicates that individual responses to those concepts differ from participant to participant. While all participants can attest to similar experiences or emotions, their responses vary. Personal experience and individual characteristics can attribute to the variance in responses. An event such as negotiating an immigration checkpoint can elicit different responses by individuals in the participant pool, consequently situating them on the different quadrants.

The most considerable finding of this research, however, lies in the fact that while individual participants navigate a dominant quadrant produced by their particular social and legal dimensions, what actually occurs is a constant navigation of dimensions created by social and legal spaces. Unauthorized students navigate from an explicit to an implicit lived space and from a regulated to an unregulated legal space continuously. The researcher proposes that the negotiation of lived spaces of unauthorized youth may be properly defined as a multidimensional paradigm where the negotiation of legal and social spaces is elastic and fluid.

Chapter 7

Discussion, Implications, and Recommendations

This chapter provides a reflection of the study from the researcher's perspective and recommendations for further research. The chapter begins with a discussion of the findings that yielded information on the main research question of the study. In addition, the researcher discusses the implications of the findings with the need to invest in unauthorized youth who not only excel in high school, but are completing their college degrees. Finally, recommendations for further research are provided.

The Research Question

Chapter four of the study described the findings to the three sub-questions that examined data to inform the main question of the study. The research question of this study asked: What are the existing socio-psychological forces that shape the daily-lived experiences and negotiated spaces of un-authorized youth pursuing access to higher education in the United States? By answering the main question of the study a clear picture of the negotia-tion of lived spaces by college-aged unauthorized youth emerged.

The findings of the study suggest eight themes that described the socio-psychological forces that shape the daily lived experiences of unauthor-ized college-age youth. These themes are: Micro-agressions, Identity and Belonging; Trauma; Resiliency, Adaptability, and Pragmatism; Member-ship; Agency; Family; and Structural Violence. Furthermore, four concepts described how the participants navigate their regulated and unregulated lived space, namely, living in Ambivalence, Encapsulation, Dissonance, and Rejection.

The types of daily-lived situations that confront the undocumented youths' sense of identity and belonging include what for most Americans are ordinary everyday activities that an individual may partake in, such as going to school, driving, shopping, attending social events, recreational activities, or interacting with others in selected parts within their community. While for most people such activities would appear routine and mundane, in the undocumented youth experience such activities produce tensions that need to be negotiated daily.

Consider driving, an activity that every young teenagers dreams about. Driving has become heavily politicized in the United States in recent years with numerous states denying the unauthorized population a driver's license. The impact of not having a driver's license goes far beyond not being able to drive a vehicle. In a culture where a driver's license has become consistent with identity, to be denied one is analogous to denying membership or even legal existence. The impact of not having an identity ranges from the denial of gym memberships to being locked out from such a fundamental component of the American economy as credit.

The denial of membership to a gym might appear to some as insignificant. Such rejection, however, goes beyond the seeking of fitness. Membership denial to a gym based on the lack of valid forms of identification transcends into the realms of inclusive and exclusionary policy in a society. In other words, who can become a member of a group, and how can the privilege of membership be proven resides in one's ability to have legal identification. In the United States a social security number or another preferred form of identification of membership is imperative. Unauthorized college-aged students possess neither.

Being consistently on the alert wherever they are is part of everyday reality for the unauthorized youth in the United States. This alertness, however, is not without consequences. The reality of living always vigilant of their surroundings, adapting to restrictions by legal conditions, and negotiating the conflict produced by their legal status generates trauma.

Living always wary of one's surroundings can be emotionally draining and psychologically distressing. Various types of psychological trauma impact how undocumented youth negotiate their daily-lived situations. Trauma has been defined in this study from a psychological perspective as the feeling of fear, stress, depression, exclusion, and apprehension as a result of having unauthorized legal status.

The participants of this study have all been impacted emotionally by their legal status in the United States. They have all at one time or another experienced the fear of being apprehended and deported. Most have vivid memories of crossing the border and of loved ones being apprehended. Deportation for them would mean the end of all their hard work, dreams, and aspirations. It would mean the separation from their family and forceful adaptation to a country that, while they were born there, they know little about.

It is at the very least ironic that most of the participants while expressing love for their country of birth, if deported would feel "alien" in Mexico. Their lives since childhood have been formed in the United States. To think they can be exiled from the place they have always known as home causes fear and depression. Participants in the study reported lack of sleep and deficient concentration when confronted with the possibility of deportation.

Adding to the fear and emotional stress is the constant exposure to micro aggressions from a society that, while seeing itself as humanitarian and the product of an immigrant experience, is nativist and detached. Prejudice and fear permeate and are disseminated through public commentary and/or the national media. Federal, state, and local governments do little to alleviate the social tensions that are promoted through stereotypes and statistics that replace the existing conditions and humanity of children.

To respond to the daily psychological trauma that they experience, Latino undocumented youth create an array of coping skills. Coping skills, as defined in this study, are the various ways an individual positively or negatively confronts complex situations produced by their illegal status. Latino undocumented youth often respond to the daily psychological trauma that they experience with pragmatism, incredible adaptability, and resiliency.

Confronted with legal, financial, and other social obstacles, they are consistently constructing ways to create support systems and find avenues and spaces where they can not only exist but thrive. The very fact that they are enrolled in colleges and universities speaks volumes about the resiliency of these youth. Finding ways to earn money for college, arranging transportation, and learning who to trust are but a few of the adaptive ways the unauthorized youth cope with their reality.

Long lasting tribulations associated with structural violence are a constant challenge in the lives of unauthorized youth. Services and guarantees allocated to most Americans and to students in particular are within reach of the undocumented scholar but unavailable to them. Often these are vital safety nets that may even save lives. Access to health care, psychological counseling, even protection by law enforcement are often seen not as avenues of assistance but as a means of possible detection of their illegal status and thus deportation.

Family and friends have been for most of the participants in the study the source of strength and the base from which their quest for higher education emanates. The family nucleus appears to be the centerpiece in many of these otherwise "American" success stories. Sadly, family values as the centerpiece of American and Christian ideals in this country are overlooked where legal status is concerned.

Despite the many obstacles faced by these youth, one finds them resilient and unwilling to be denied their future and very determined to succeed. They understand the value of higher education and are hopeful that the laws of this country will allow them to live out of the shadows. Waiting for change, they navigate the parameters constructed by the legal and explicit and implicit lived space dimensions. The constant navigation of lived spaces creates experiences of ambivalence, encapsulation, dissonance, and rejection.

Ambivalence is the product of spaces where both safety and danger could be at hand. Ambivalence is a state of living in a part of the community where, while experiencing a sense of ease, there also exists constant apprehension or trauma associated with not being legal, and thus one lives under stress. Involvement in such activities include going to local stores, church functions, or family gatherings such as in a park that are enjoyed, but not without the fear of possible legal ramifications.

Encapsulation is dominated by fear and apprehension. Encapsulation is a state of constant fear known only to the individual or intimates others. Teachers, peers, and fellow students are unaware of the legal status of the person. Consequently, a school fieldtrip, designed to be instructive and enjoyable, can extract feelings of fear and apprehension in the unauthorized student, given that legal and disclosure barriers may be present.

Dissonance is incongruence or contradictory cognition. This state of dissonance is defined as trauma experienced in the form of depression, and the feeling of being out of harmony with one's surroundings. Dissonance, thus, is a state of living in trauma and out of harmony within the community and within the self. For the participants of the study, the inability to share the legal status with others creates an inner conflict, a feeling of helplessness, and often depression. A simple college night out with friends to local establishments that require a driver's license for identification becomes an emotional test for unauthorized individuals.

Rejection is the product of exclusion from social integration and social identity. Here the individual suffers the trauma of having no legal guarantee of being treated fairly and within the law and feeling excluded socially and from being integrated into the community or having a civil social identity.

Because of their illegal status, the eight college-age unauthorized youth have lived their lives bounded by social-psychological forces that shape their daily-lived experiences, and they have been forced to consistently negotiate social and legal spaces. The legal and political conditions have catapulted these youth into an arena where they have to negotiate the tensions produced by their official status.

This study has examined the lived spaces of selected unauthorized college-aged youth. These youth on a daily basis confront their sense of identity, belonging, psychological emotions, and living space. The voices, issues, fears, trauma found in the autobiographies, interviews, and face-to-face dialogues led the researcher to suggest the following framework for illustrating the daily psychological trauma experienced by college-age unauthorized students as they negotiate their daily-lived situations.

In synthesis, the conceptual framework serves as a proposed tool to analyze the explicit and implicit (see Figure 7.1) lived spaces of unauthorized Latino youth living in the United States and how the tensions of not residing legally in the immediate and broader spaces of the community, state, and nation are negotiated.

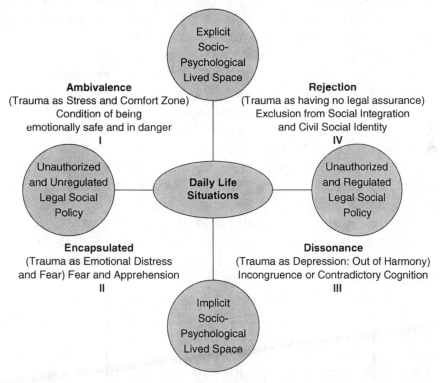

Figure 7.1 Conceptual framework for understanding the socio-psychology of lived spaces and regulated social policy in residing in the United States.

Discussions and Implications

The study has been emotionally demanding as well as rewarding. As the researcher, I sincerely hope that it is fruitful in advancing the discourse over the status of the unauthorized student population, their lives, and their aspirations. The lives and dreams of the participants highlight an array of the socio-psychological and economic challenges that need to be met. But their pragmatism and agency also offer a ray of hope.

The challenges for the researcher come from bearing witness to the desperation of the unauthorized college-age student population, so much desire to succeed, such a need to belong, and few stakeholders who will listen. Over the last few years my disillusion with the immigration policy and lack of humanity in the United States has multiplied. What we as a country do to these young people is simply inhumane and emotionally and psychologically violent.

At the same time, however, the struggle of the young people I met have renewed my hope in the human spirit. For, just like a flower that blooms in the desert, they are resilient, hopeful, and determined to succeed. We should be applauding their commitment, supporting their growth, and have young children follow their example of self-determination and personal growth to attain a college degree and contribute back to society.

To ignore and not address this population is simply wrong and counterproductive. To those who are concerned with the development of the human condition, the pushing forward of the discourse over access to higher education by undocumented students is essential. As it has been reported in this study, the numbers alone demand a dialogue.

Specifically, in mid-2005 it was estimated that there were some two million undocumented children in schools in the United States and with an estimated 65,000 graduating from high school every year (Horwedel, 2006). It is also estimated that there are some 50,000 undocumented students in United States colleges (Horwedel, 2006). If we consider that 57 percent of the general undocumented populations are Mexican nationals, we may deduce that Mexican undocumented youth are highly represented in this group (Diaz-Strong and Meiners, 2007).

Another intent of this study was to provide insight into the lives, aspirations, and resiliency of the unauthorized student population pursuing a college degree in the United States. Scholars, educators, immigration reform advocates, and those against immigration reform can reflect on the conditions and personal trauma experienced by college-aged unauthorized students. This insight may lead to more-informed positions and reforms in educational, social, and immigration policy.

In the last few years, the issue of higher education for undocumented high school graduates has increasingly gained attention in the United States. Several states have passed laws to give these students access to college at in-state tuition rates, but federal regulations limit their access to financial aid. Education and immigration advocates, as well as immigrant students, are pushing to widen the access to public colleges and universities nationwide (Vock, 2008; Jefferies, 2007).

In California, Assembly Bill 540 of 2001 allows immigrant students to pay in-state tuition if they meet a set of requirements. To qualify, a student must have attended a California high school for three or more years. Students must have a California high school diploma or GED. They must sign a statement with the school, stating that he/she will apply for legal residency as soon as they are eligible to do so. Through this bill undocumented students can register or be enrolled in California Community College, California State University, or University of California campuses. This AB 540 legislation has created uproar in many American communities who see such laws as pandering to illegal aliens (Jefferies, 2007).

Efforts to change biased laws and regulations controlling access to higher education are not without controversy. Opposition often fueled by blatant discrimination is widespread. Unauthorized immigrants face increasing attacks by governmental legislation and enforcement. As in the past, people hold immigrants responsible for economic woes in the U.S. (Bingham, 2003; Acuna, 2007).

The recent failures of immigration reform, including the nationally proposed Dream Act of 2003, serve as testimony to such divergence. The derailing of the Dream Act alienated a young population as their legal and academic status continues to be unresolved. The Dream Act was proposed through federal legislation that was designed to grant high school students with good academic standing legal status in the United States. Legal status would also be extended to undocumented immigrants of good moral character who wanted to serve in the armed forces or attend college.

In the larger context, American immigration policy needs to be analyzed and reformed. Unauthorized immigration is something that most citizens of the United States wish was stopped and immigration laws enforced. The influx of inexpensive labor for American corporate interest and economic remittance to Mexico far exceed what the popular position assumes.

Likewise, the American consumer culture must acknowledge responsibility. Most Americans see immigration as one-dimensional in terms of its cause and take no accountability for its existence. The push and pull factors created by American foreign policy and the demands of American markets are ignored by most. Simply put, American demands for goods and services create an economic vortex that pulls immigration into the United States. This is particularly true of undocumented immigration.

For the researcher, the answer is clear. We must take responsibility as Americans and as consumers for immigration, including the presence of unauthorized children.

Recommendation for Further Research

The researcher proposes that further study focusing in unauthorized college-age students is needed. Several suggestions are put forward here.

First, a study of the unauthorized student population with a larger participant pool would be imperative to further test the framework of the study and the themes produced. Given the existing population of college-age unauthorized youth pursuing an education, it is reasonable to suggest that studies where the participant pool ranges in the thousands.

Second, undertake a study that encompasses a larger geographical area to indicate if any differences exist in the different regions of the country. The contrast between border cities where the political climate over immigration is often more tense with cities such as Los Angeles, Houston, Chicago, Miami, and New York would be particularly insightful.

Third, a future study should investigate the impact of gender and class. What is the role of class on the adaptation to the reality of the undocumented youth population? What role does gender play in adjusting to the pressures of unauthorized status in the United States? These are important questions that need to be answered.

Fourth, the study of other ethnically diverse student immigrant groups would be essential. What are the differences and similarities and negotiating lived situations between Latino origin and non-Latino origin populations? Some governmental agencies report that half of the unauthorized population is composed of non-Mexican-origin populace. Analyses of Chinese, Brazilian, Somalia, Ethiopian, and other unauthorized population would be of value.

Fifth, future research can focus on the experiences between four-year college and community college populations to see if different social and economic tools and lived strategies are used to negotiate the lived situations by unauthorized youth. The explicit and implicit cost of education and the impact of accessibility could be analyzed within this study.

Sixth, as a study that examines if and/or how colleges and universities provide spaces and information were the unauthorized student can find safety and learn of their rights and the existing avenues to complete graduation requirements is essential. It is painfully clear from this study that most participants were unaware of their rights or options as unauthorized students in a community college or university.

Seventh, a study that examines the availability and support to address the trauma (social, psychological, political, and economic) that is lived/experienced by undocumented college-age students would provide insights as to the humanity of our society.

Last, the eighth recommendation calls for the federal government to create a viable path to legal status for undocumented youth in general, and specifically those in college who directly contribute to the social cultural capital of this nation. An overhaul of the American immigration policy in general is needed. A policy that addresses the lives of these youth, however, is a must; it is the humane thing to do.

REFERENCES

Acuña, R. (2007). *Occupied America: A History of Chicanos* (5th Ed.). London: Pearson.

Auerbach, E. (2003). Mimesis: *The Representation of Reality in Western Literature* (Deluxe Ed.). Princeton: Princeton University Press.

Anyon, J. (2005). *Radical Possibilities. Basic Facts About In-state Tuition for Undocumented Immigrant Students.* New York: Routledge.

Balderrama, E.B., and R. Rodriguez. (1995). *Decade of Betrayal: Mexican Repatriation in the 1930s* (1st Ed.). Albuquerque: University of New Mexico Press.

Behavenet. (2000). DSM-IV Diagnostic Criteria for 309.81 Posttraumatic Stress Disorder from <http://www.behavenet.com/capsules/disorders/ptsd.htm>.

Bingman, R.R. (2003). *Aztlan: Conspiracy to Overthrow the American Southwest by Force!* [Electronic Version]. *No B.S. News Magazine* from http://www.criminalgovernment.com/ docs/rel/atzlan_ot.html.

Capps, R., R.A. Castaneda, A. Chaundy, and R. Santos. (2007). *Paying the Price: The Impact of Immigration Raids on America's Children* from http://www.nclr.org/content/publications.

Charmaz, K. (2005). *Constructing Grounded Theory: A Practical Guide Through Qualitative Analysis.* Thousand Oaks, CA: Sage Publications.

Chavez, R.L. (1991). *Shadowed Lives: Undocumented Immigrants in American Society.* Stanford, CA: Stanford Press.

Clandinin, D.J., and F.M. Connelly. (1991). Narrative and Story in Practice and Research. In D.A. Schon (Ed.). *The Reflective Turn* (pp. 258–281). New York: Teachers College Press.

Clandinin, D.J., and F.M. Connelly. (1994). Personal Experience Methods. In N.K. Denzin and Y.S. Lincoln (Eds.). *Handbook of Qualitative Research* (pp. 413–427). Thousand Oaks, CA: Sage Publications.

Connelly, F.M., and J, Clandinin. (2004). *Narrative Inquiry: Experience and Story in Qualitative Research.* Hoboken, NJ: Wiley, John & Sons.

Cortese, A. (2003). *Teachers Self Knowledge of Their Personal and Professional Epistemologies as Seen Through Teaching.* Unpublished doctoral dissertation. San Diego State University-Claremont Graduate Doctoral Program.

Darder, A., R.D. Torres, and H.Gutâierrez, (1997). *Latinos and Education: A Critical Reader.* New York: Routledge.

de la Cruz, G.P., and R.R. Ramirez. (June 2003). *The Hispanic Population in the United States March 2002* (Report). Washington DC: U.S. Department of Commerce, U.S. Census Bureau.

Denzin, N.K., and Y.S. Lincoln. (2000). *Handbook of Qualitative Research* (2nd Ed.). Thousand Oaks, CA: Sage Publications.

Diaz-Strong, D., and E. Meiners. (2007). *Residents, Alien Policies, and Resistances: Experiences of Undocumented Latina/o Students in Chicago's Colleges and Universities.* InterActions: *UCLA Journal of Education and Information Studies,* 3(2).

Dozier, S.B. (2001). *Undocumented and Documented International Students: Comparative Study of Their Academic Performance* from [Electronic version]. *Community College Review,* 29:43–53.

Gaona, E. (2006, April 2, 2006). Protest, Celebration Mingle. *San Diego Union–Tribune,* pp. 2, 5.

García, I.M. (1997). *Chicanismo: The Forging of a Militant Ethos Among Mexican Americans.* Tucson: University of Arizona Press.

Geisler, J.S. (1968). *The Effects of a Compensatory Education Program on the Self-concept and Achievement of High School Age Youth from Low Income Families.* Unpublished Thesis Ph D. University of Toledo 1968.

Griswold, D.R. (2008). *Chicano San Diego: Cultural Space and the Struggle for Justice.* Tucson: The University of Arizona Press.

Gutierrez, C.G. (1999). Fostering Identity: Mexico's Relations with Its Diaspora. *The Journal of American History,* 86(2):545–567.

Gutierrez, D.G. (1999). Migration, Emergent Ethnicity, and the "Third Space": The Shifting Politics of Nationalism in Greater Mexico. *The Journal of American History,* 86(2):481–517.

Hanley, M.S. (2002). *The Scope of Multicultural Education.* New Horizons for Learning, from http://www.newhorizons.org/strategies/multicultural/hanley.htm.

Hirsch, H., and A. Gutierrez. (1977). *Learning to Be Militant: Ethnic Identity and the Development of Political Militancy in a Chicano Community.* San Francisco: R & E Research Associates.

Horwedel, M.D. (2006). *For Illegal College Students, An Uncertain Future.* Retrieved 4/22/08 from www.diverseeducation.com/artman/publish/printer_5815.shtml.

Jacobo, J.R. (2006). *Frontera del Norte: Readings in Chicano and Border History* (3rd. Ed.). San Diego, CA: Southern Border Press.

Jacobo, R., M. Flores, and M. Correa. (2003). *The Giving Gaze: An Intimate Topography of the Border.* San Diego CA: Larc Press.

Krug, M. (1971). *Cultural Pluralism in a Historical Perspective.* Institute for Cultural Pluralism, San Diego State University, 29.

Larralde, C., and R. Jacobo. (2000). *Juan Cortina and the Struggle for Justice in Texas.* Dubuque, IA: Kendall/Hunt.

Leininger, M. (1992). *Current Issues, Problems, and Trends to Advance Qualitative Paradigmatic Research Methods.* Thousand Oaks, CA: Sage Publications.

Lemert, C. (2003). *The Analytic Foundations of Social Violence.* Mod. Psychoanal., 28: 217–234.

Magee, M., H. Gao, and E. Fitzsimons. (April 1, 2006). A Protest Unmatched in Magnitutde, Civility. *The San Diego Union Tribune*, pp. 1, 16.

Mariscal, J. (2006, March 31). The Sleeping Giant Awakens Again. *San Diego Union Tribune*, p. 9.

McAdoo, H.P. (1999). *Family Ethnicity: Strength in Diversity* (2nd Ed.). Thousand Oaks, CA: Sage Publications.

McDaniel, E.L. (1967). *Relationships Between Self-concept and Specific Variables in a Low-income Culturally Different Population.* Unpublished Thesis Ph.D. University of Austin, 1967.

McWilliams, C., and M.S. Meier. (1990). *North from Mexico: the Spanish-speaking People of the United States* (New Ed.). New York: Greenwood Press.

Merton, R.K. (1957). *Social Theory and the Social Structure.* New York: Free Press of Glencoe.

Meyer, M.C., and W.H. Beezley. (2000). The Oxford History of Mexico. Oxford; New York: Oxford University Press.

Miles, J. (1992, October). Blacks vs. Browns *The Atlantic Monthly*, 270:41.

Mora, J.M., and D.R. Diaz. (2004). *Latino Social Policy: A Participatory Research Model.* New York: Haworth Press.

Moran, C. (2006, Apr. 1). First Walkouts Transform into Variety of Reactions. *San Diego Union-Tribune*, pp. 1, 16.

National Institute of Mental Health. (1984). *Mexican Origin People in the United States*: Austin (Texas) Pilot Survey, 1978–1979. from http://www.icpsr.umich.edu/access/ index.html.

National Institute of Public Health. (2008, Apr. 2). Post-Traumatic Stress Disorder (PTSD) from <http://www.nimh.nih.gov/health/topics/post-traumatic-stress-disorder-ptsd/ index.shtml>.

Oboler, S. (1995). *Ethnic Labels, Latino Lives: Identity and the Politics of (Re) Presentation in the United States.* Minneapolis: University of Minnesota Press.

Ornelas, Michael. (2000). *Between the Conquest: Readings in Early Chicano Historical Experience* (3rd Ed.). Dubuque: Kendall/Hunt.

Padilla, A.M. (1995). *Hispanic Psychology: Critical Issues in Theory and Research.* Thousand Oaks, CA: Sage Publications.

Peäna, D.G. (1998). *Chicano Culture, Ecology, Politics: Subversive Kin.* Tucson: University of Arizona Press.

Pizarro, M. (2005). *Chicanas and Chicanos in School: Racial Profiling, Identity Battles, and Empowerment* (1st Ed.). Austin, TX: University of Texas Press.

Plotnik, R. (2005). Introduction to Psychology. Thomson-Wadsworth 21:491 *Plyer v. Doe* 457 US 202 (1982).

Renterâia, T.H. (1998). *Chicano Professionals: Culture, Conflict, and Identity*. New York: Garland Publications.

Rodrâiguez, S. (1986). *The Hispano Homeland Debate*. Stanford, CA: Stanford Center for Chicano Research.

Rosaldo, R., W.V. Flores, and B.G. Silvestrini. (1994). *Identity, Conflict, and Evolving Latino Communities: Cultural Citizenship in San Jose, California*. Stanford, CA: Stanford Center for Chicano Research.

Schemmel, D.R. (1969). *The Construction of the Vocational Aspiration-Expectation Index for Low-income Parents and Its Relationship with Academic Achievement of Early Elementary Children*. Unpublished Thesis Ph.D. Ohio University, 1969.

Soja, W.E. (2007). *Journey to Los Angeles and Other Real and Imagined Places*. Maryland: Blackwell.

Solorzano, D., M. Ceja, and T. Yosso. (2000). Critical Race Theory, Racial Microaggressions and Campus Racial Climate: The Experiences of African American College Students. *Journal of Negro Education*, 69:60–73.

Solorzano, D. (1997). Images and Words That Wound: Critical Race Theory, Racial Stereotyping, and Teacher Education. *Teacher Education Quarterly*, 24:5–19.

United States Department of Commerce. Bureau of the Census. (1984a). Census of Population and Housing United States, 1970 Public Use Sample: Modified 1/1000 15% State Samples. from http://www.icpsr.umich.edu/access/index.html.

Velez-Ibanez, C.C. (1996) *Border Visions: Mexican Cultures of the Southwest United States*. Tucson: The University of Arizona.

Valdez, E.O. (1991). *Division of Labor and Well-being in Dual-income Chicano Families*. Unpublished Thesis Ph.D. University of California Riverside, 1991.

Vazquez, F.H., and R.D. Torres, (2003). *Latino/a Thought: Culture, Politics, and Society*. Lanham, MD: Rowman & Littlefield.

Villarreal, R.E. (1979). *Chicano Elites and Non-elites: An Inquiry into Social and Political Change*. Palo Alto, CA: R & E Research Associates.

World Psychiatry. (2005) February; 4(1):18–24. Bhugra, Dinish and Becker, Mathew. Migration, Cultural Bereavement and Cultural Identity. PubMed PMCID: PMC1414713 from <http://www.pubmedcentral.nih.gov/articlerender.fcgi?artid=1414713>.

Yin, R.K. (1984). *Case Study Research: Design and Methods*. Thousand Oaks, CA: Sage Publications.

Zamoff, B.R. (1968). *A Pre-college Program for Lower Income Youth: An Analysis of "Upward Bound" Students*. Unpublished Thesis Ph.D. Columbia University 1968.

Zinn, H. (2003). *A Peoples History of the United States: Volume II. The Civil War to the Present*. New York: The New Press.

Appendix A

San Diego State University Consent to Act as a Research Study

The Negotiation of Lived Spaces by Unauthorized College-Aged Youth

You are being asked to participate in a research study. Before you give your consent to volunteer, it is important that you read the following information and ask as many questions as necessary to be sure you understand what you will be asked to do.

Investigators: My name is Rodolfo Jacobo Jr. I am working on my dissertation in the San Diego State University/Claremont Graduate University Joint Doctoral Program in Education. I will be the researcher under the direction of Dr. Alberto Ochoa of the SDSU College of Education.

Purpose of the Study: I am conducting research on the unauthorized student population pursuing a college degree in the United States. I am interested in learning more about their lives, aspirations, and resiliency. The main objective is to study how the unauthorized student population has had to adjust to the reality of living illegally in the United States. Eight participants will be included in this study. You are eligible to participate if:

- You are bilingual, bicultural, and bi-literate, and of Latino origin
- You do not have the right to live in the U.S. (illegal status)
- You are enrolled full-time in college
- You are over the age of eighteen
- You have resided illegally in the United Sates for most of your life

Description of the Study: To determine if you are eligible to participate, you will be asked to complete a preliminary screening questionnaire to ensure that you meet the criteria mentioned above. If your responses indicate that you are eligible, you will be asked to meet with the researcher at a location and time of your choosing. If you are not eligible to participate, the information obtained from you during screening will be omitted from this study and shredded to protect your privacy.

If you are eligible to participate, you will complete the following tasks:

- Meet a total of three times with the researcher at a location and time of your choosing. Each meeting will take one hour.
- Write an autobiography no more than twenty pages within a month of the first meeting. You will be asked to write about how being undocumented in the United States has impacted your life. What have been the challenges and the limitations, and how have you overcome them? What are your aspirations and your fears?
- The study will last up to six weeks. Participants will be given a month to complete autobiographies.

Risks or Discomforts: You may feel worried that participation in this study may allow someone to find out about your illegal status in this country. The researcher will do his best to keep all of the information you provide during this study private. The researcher will create a code/pseudonym that is linked to your name only on a master list that will be stored separately from all study data. Only members of the research team will have access to the master list. All interview data and autobiographies are labeled with only this code/pseudonym. Once all data are collected, the master list linking names and code/pseudonym will be destroyed.

Participation in this study may also cause you to feel emotional stress associated with the recollection of emotional traumatic moments. You may withdraw from the study at any time if you begin to feel upset. I also have a list of confidential counseling resources that I can provide you with if you would like to talk to a professional about your feelings.

Benefits of the Study: It is hoped that this study will provide insight into the unauthorized student population pursuing a college degree in the United States. Scholars, educators, immigration reform advocates, and those against. This insight may lead to more informed positions and reforms in educational, social, and immigration policy. I cannot guarantee, however, that you will receive any benefits from participating in this study.

Confidentiality: Confidentiality will be maintained to the extent allowed by law. The researcher will create a code/pseudonym that is linked to the participant's name on a master list stored separately from all study data. All interview data and autobiographies are labeled with only the code/pseudonym. Once all data are collected, the master list linking names and code/pseudonym will be destroyed.

Costs and/or Compensation for Participation: There are no costs associated with participation in this study. Any cost associated with meeting with the researcher, such as transportation, or meals, will be covered by the researcher of the study.

Voluntary Nature of Participation: Participation in this study is voluntary. Your choice of whether or not to participate will not influence your future relations with San Diego State University. If you decide to participate, you are free to withdraw your consent and to stop your participation at any time without penalty or loss of benefits to which you are allowed.

Questions about the Study: If you have any questions about the research now, please ask. If you have any questions later about the research, please contact me at 619.540-5610 or rjacobo@mail.sdsu.edu.

If you have any questions about your rights as a participant in this study, you may contact the Institutional Review Board at San Diego State University (telephone: 619-594-6622; email: irb@mail.sdsu.edu).

Consent to Participate: Your signature below indicates that you have read the information in this document and have had a chance to ask any questions you have about the study. Your signature also indicates that you agree to be in the study and have been told that you can change your mind and withdraw your consent to participate at any time. You have been given a copy of this consent form, and you have been told that by signing this consent form you are not giving up any of your legal rights.

You also have the option of not signing this form. You can still participate in this study even if you do not sign the consent, as long as you verbally acknowledge that you have received the information needed to make an informed choice to participate in the study. With or without a signature, you will receive a copy of this form.

_____

Name of Participant (please print)

_____   _____

Signature of Participant   Date

_____   _____

Signature of Investigator   Date

Appendix B

Information on Research Study on the Undocumented College Student Experience

Student Volunteers are needed for a dissertation study on the college experiences of undocumented college students. The main objective is to study how the undocumented student population has had to adjust to the reality of being college students in the United States.

Willing participants who meet the following criteria are sought for the study:

a. Participants must be bilingual, bicultural and bi-literate, and of Latino origin.
b. Participant must have lived in the United States since childhood.
c. Participants must be enrolled full-time in a community college or university.
d. Participants must not have the legal right to live in the U.S. (illegal status).
e. Participants must be eighteen years or older.

If you decide to participate, please note:

- Your participation in this study is completely voluntary.
- Participants will be protected by confidential procedures and data security. The researcher will create a code/pseudonym that is linked to the participant's name on a master list stored separately from all study data. All interview data and autobiographies are labeled with only the code/pseudonym. Once all data are collected, the master list linking names and code/pseudonym will be destroyed.
- You have the right to stop your participation at any time.

Description of the Study

1. Meet a total of three times with the researcher at a location and time of your choosing. Each meeting will take one hour.

2. Write an autobiography no more than twenty pages within a month of the first meeting. You will be asked to write about how being undocumented in the United States has impacted your life. What have been the challenges and the limitations, and how have you overcome them? What are your aspirations and your fears?
3. The study will last up to six weeks. Participants will be given a month to complete autobiographies.

Questions about the Study

If you have any questions regarding this survey, please contact me at 619.540-5610 or rjacobo@mail.sdsu.edu. You may also contact the Institutional Review Board at SDSU (619-594-6622) to report problems or concerns related to this study. If you have any questions about your rights as a participant in this study, you may contact the Institutional Review Board at San Diego State University (telephone: 619-594-6622; email: irb@mail.sdsu.edu).

Initial Screening Process Form

Research Code: _____

1. Where were you born? _____
   _____

2. At what age did you come to the United States? _____
   _____

3. Did you enter the United States legally?

   YES   NO

   If Yes, what type of legal document did you have?

   _____

4. Do you currently reside legally in the United States?

   YES   NO

5. How many years have you lived in the United States illegally?
   _____

6. What was the first grade level of education you entered in the United States? _____

7. Did you attend at least three years of high school in California?

   YES   NO

8. Are you the age of 18 or older?

   YES   NO

9. Are you currently enrolled full time in college or university?

   YES   NO

10. Are you an AB540 student?

    YES   NO

Negotiation of Lived Space: Guiding Questions

Semi-structure interview

1. Where is your family from?
2. At what age did you come to the United States?
3. What do you know as to why your family and/or parents moved to the U.S.?
4. When did you first become aware of your legal status?
5. How has your legal status affect you as a child? In your youth (teenage years)? In your present stage of your life? What can you recall about your experiences in elementary school? In middle school? In high school? In college?
6. How did your legal status affect you in the different stages of your education?
7. Given your legal status:

   When do you feel safe?

   Where do you feel safe?

   When do you not feel safe?

   Where do you not feel safe?
8. How has the being undocumented affected how you see yourself?

   As child?

   In your teenage years?

   As a college student?
9. What things or events make you feel like you do not belong in the United States?
10. What are the types of concerns that you have every day?

11. How do undocumented youth respond to the concerns and stress that are experienced on a daily basis?

12. In general, what makes you keep going with your life? What are your aspirations? Do you think you are resilient?

Trangulation Case Study Sample

Once the selection process and informed consent procedures had been executed, data was gathered. The first step in the process of gathering data was a face-to-face semi-structured interview. The questions in Appendix E were used to obtain information on the negotiation of lived space for each of the eight participants. With consent permission, the interviews were documented and transcribed, all the while using their pseudonym. This appendix serves an example of one document source for identifying the descriptors supporting the themes highlighted in this study.

Semi-Structured Interview

1. Where is your family from?
   a. My family is from Jalisco, Mexico

2. At what age did you come to the United States?
   a. I was just <u>one year old when I came to this country.</u>

3. What do you know as to why your family and/or parents moved to the U.S.?
   a. We were very poor; my <u>father had no work and mother washed other</u> <u>people's clothes</u> to make ends meet, but it was never enough.

4. When did you first become aware of your legal status?
   a. It was in high school. When all my classmates talked about going to college, I started making plans. When I told my mother, she told me <u>I was not going to able to go to college.</u> That was when <u>I first realized I was not legal.</u> It was a very sad day for me. I remember that <u>I cried.</u>

5. How has your legal status affect you as a child? In your youth (teenage years)?
   a. I quickly realized why things were the way that they were. I realized why all the limitations existed. As children <u>we could not go south and we could not go too north. In fact we never went anywhere. I have never met my grandparents and family who are in Mexico.</u>

6. In you present stage of your life as a college student?
   a. Not having legal status means <u>I cannot get any form of assistance to go to college.</u> I have to work in order to pay for my classes. Since <u>I do not have a social security number, the only jobs I get are low-paid and often abusive.</u> My mother can only do so much because she is here illegally too. <u>Only my sisters are legally here because they were all born here.</u> I hope they take advantage of what they have.

7. Can you recall any positive or negative experiences in elementary school? In middle school? In high school? In college?
   a. I just recall having <u>dreams of becoming a business woman</u> and helping my mother out. For many years we lived in an abandon house with no lights or water. <u>High school was a challenge, it was</u>

not easy been bused from the barrio to a rich school to begin with, and when I found out I was illegal, well, my dreams crumbled. But I have to say my mother has always being a great mother and she has sacrificed everything for us.

8. Specifically, how did your legal status affect you in the different stages of your education?
   a. Well, it sets a lot of <u>limitations</u> on what you can do, where you can go to college, and what you major in. All students choose; <u>we have few, if any, choices.</u>

9. Given your daily-lived situations and experiences, what are the comfort zones of your daily-lived situations? What are the uncomfortable confrontation zones of your daily-lived situations?
   a. The <u>comfort zones are my family and friends.</u> As I said before, my mother is the best mother I could ask for. <u>Many of my friends are either here illegally themselves or they have a family member in the same situation, so we understand the situation. Our neighborhood is overall safe; we rarely venture out. We go to church, to the laundry, and the park. Our only concern is when we go out. The bus and the trolley are dangerous; we always worry about our mom one day not coming back.</u>

10. Did the status of being undocumented affect your sense of identity (how you identify yourself) as a child? In your teenage years? As a college student?
    a. Yes, it does. <u>It makes one feel like one does not belong, like there is something bad with us, like we have no rights. Those feelings of</u>

<u>fear and frustration get bigger as one gets older.</u> As child things seem different than as an adult.

11. What are the types of daily-lived situations that you confront as undocumented youth? In your younger years, what was your sense of belonging?
   a. Like I was saying, when you are younger things are different. If you asked me as a child that question, I would answer, I was my mother's child and that is where I belonged. <u>As adult things are different; can't I say I am Mexican if I did not live there much? I have been here 99% of my life and I cannot say I am an American.</u> Does that make sense?

12. What are the types of concerns that impact you directly as an undocumented youth negotiating your daily-lived situations?
   a. I <u>worry about my mother.</u> I worry that one day as she goes off to work to clean houses, <u>she might not come back.</u> The <u>immigration</u> often <u>patrols the trolley and the bus.</u> <u>We sometimes have nightmare about that.</u>

13. How did you as an undocumented youth respond to the daily concerns and stress that you experienced on a daily basis?
   a. <u>We pray a lot. We also take precautions</u> in the trolley or in the bus. Most of all, despite it all, we try to have fun and laugh a lot. We cannot do much more but <u>hope the law will change.</u>

14. In general, what makes you keep going in life? What are your aspirations? Do you think you are resilient (willing to forge ahead)?
    a. I think I am that (resilient), but sometimes <u>I do get sad and cry</u>. I hope the law will change.
    I want to study and help my <u>family live a better life.</u> What <u>I want the most is a green card.</u>

15. Any other thought you wish to add, expand, or clarify on the challenges facing college-aged youth?
    a. No, thank you, and I hope it helps others as well as us. Let me know if you want to meet again.

Autobiography

The second phase used an autobiographical approach to allow the participants to write autobiographies while providing each participant with free reign of their narrative on their lived unauthorized experiences.

Early Years

My name is Brenda. <u>I was born in Guadalajara, Jalisco, Mexico.</u> I hear it's a beautiful city, but the truth is, I don't know this city at all. <u>I only lived there the first few months of my life.</u> Now I am twenty years old living in the beautiful city of San Diego. My parents brought me here at the age of eleven months. I don't remember this, but I heard from my parents that we <u>crossed over through "El Cerro" or the hills.</u> Back then they say everything was much simpler.

Elementary School

<u>I grew up not knowing anything about my legal status and how one day it would impact me.</u> Soon after our arrival in the United States, my little sister was born here in San Diego. Growing up, I finally had someone to play with and to fight with. It was when I would question my mom where I came from that I began to wonder. <u>I was about seven years old at the time, and I remember feeling strange because I was from somewhere else.</u> I didn't pay much attention to it, because when I would go play I would forget all about it. I remember when I was about ten years old, in elementary school, that some of the kids spoke English. I knew it was English that they were speaking because my mom had told me before what it sounded like. I <u>remember asking myself if I was ever going to learn the English language,</u> because at that time if parents wanted their children to be in Spanish-speaking only classes, they were able to do so.

Middle School

It wasn't until I was going into the sixth grade that the school district decided that all the classes were going to be English only. My mom was worried because she knew now that she was not going to be able to help us with our homework. She <u>believed that we were going to have a hard time with the schoolwork.</u> However, it wasn't as bad as she thought; I was beginning to like it and understand it. I was having fun with my friends because playing around and <u>learning English was all that mattered.</u> But time was passing us by and we only had about three months of school left. Eventually we were going to graduate from the sixth grade and go onto junior high school.

I remember being really nervous because the <u>teachers expected us to learn the material in English,</u> which of course kept me thinking a lot. It was 6 A.M., and I heard a voice calling my name, "Brenda, Brenda." I woke up and saw my mom there and she told me "Wake up, it's your first day of junior high school and you don't want to miss your bus." <u>Because I lived in Barrio Logan and attended a school at Point Loma (thirty minutes from home), I had to take the bus to school.</u>

I <u>went to school not knowing anyone; it was a different world.</u> There were plenty of older kids who went to school with me, and that scared me. I decided to do just what I needed to do. I got my schedule and waited for the bell to ring so I could go to class. I attended all my classes and made quite a few friends throughout the year. Everything was going good. It wasn't until the next year when a lot of girls didn't like me. <u>I didn't understand why they didn't like me, and I felt bad. Every single day I felt depressed because of these bullies.</u> Eventually my grades suffered, and I wasn't doing so well in school; I wouldn't even listen to the teachers. I was sent to the principal's office and then to a mentor because they did not know what to do with me.

Things began to change, and <u>Tanya, my college graduate mentor had a lot to do with it. I remember I wanted to be just like her, but I was only fourteen years old.</u> She made life seem so easy; she had a job, a car, a good boyfriend, and schooling. I liked her life a lot. When the end of the school year approached, I had to say goodbye to her. I was left alone once more, but this time it was for good. My grades went up and I was doing well again. I finally graduated from junior high.

High School

By the time I was in high <u>school, I knew how to speak and write in English,</u> so I didn't have anything to worry about. <u>It was there that the realization of inequality started. I started to see people with nice clothes, shoes, and bags. Seeing this only made me feel bad. I did not know why they had more than me. So I realized that the only way to get these things was to get a job. My mom did not have the money to pay for it because she barely had enough money to feed my sisters and me.</u>

I was doing well in school and the bulling had stopped. I was still alone, but that was okay because I wanted to focus on school. I was sixteen years old now and I was desperate to find a job. I went to look for one, but I soon received bad news from my mom. After <u>I had told my mom that I wanted to work, she told me that I was not going to have luck finding a job.</u> I couldn't get a job because I am undocumented and don't have a social security number, which is required for anyone to work legally in this country.

I remember feeling really down that day because I felt as though all my dreams were thrown out the window. That same year I met a lady named Lupita. Lupita worked at a restaurant at the time, and I had told her that I wanted to work, but I didn't have papers. She looked at me and said to me, "Do you really want to work?" I jumped with excitement, and, of course, I said yes. She told me that she had the same problem, but she was working. She got a job at that restaurant because the owner was OK with her being illegally in the country.

I was happy to know that I could do the same. I met with the owner of the restaurant, and he said he was going pay me "under the table," which meant in cash. I felt comfortable around the staff because they all spoke Spanish. I will never forget that day. But as time was going by, I started noticing things I didn't like. I was not getting paid all the hours that I worked during the week. I worked more than forty hours a week but was getting paid for far less hours. It did not seem fair, I was getting up really early to go to school and then working so many hours and yet not paid for what I had worked.

I decided to confront the owner one day and ask him why I was not getting paid all the hours that I had worked. He replied, "You have no right to tell me what to pay you because you are an illegal immigrant, and if you don't like it, I can fire you." I felt so terrible that day, and I went home crying, but I did not let my mom see me or know why I was crying. Time passed by and I quit that job, but I soon got another one similar to how I got the first one. But I was getting tired of working in food service, and I wanted something more professional.

I was seventeen during my senior year and one thing I recall was that the prom was coming up soon. Prom is so costly, so I saved for a long time. It was that same year I met a teacher named Ms. Estrada and I will never forget her. The counselors at Point Loma had accidentally placed me in her class, "Business International Trades." I felt uncomfortable because I was the only Mexican girl in the class and everyone else was white, not to mention that I didn't understand anything about business! I hated that class because everyone else seemed smarter than me, so I didn't do my work or pay attention to the lecture.

One day Ms. Estrada told me to stay after class. She told me that business was something that I should learn because in the future I was going to need it. She also boosted my confidence by telling me not to feel less, and that everyone was equal in her class. Ms. Estrada said that if I wanted to be better in life she was going to be there for me. To be honest, <u>I needed those words of encouragement because I was beginning to give up on everything.</u>

I began to understand business and found out that I was actually interested in it. I did so well that I ranked number one in that class and understood everything about business. There was one more thing that I had to complete before graduating and passing that class. <u>I had to get an internship. Luckily, I found a hotel in Downtown San Diego named the Westgate Hotel</u>. I sent my resume and a letter of recommendation from my teacher. I was really happy because I was accepted. <u>I was also happy that I could work without a social security number because I was not getting paid.</u>

I got a lot of experience <u>working there in the accounting department</u>. I realized that I liked numbers and the paperwork involved. <u>My supervisors were very pleased with my work</u> because I learned fast and did everything I was told. When my internship ended my supervisor called me in to speak with her. We sat down and talked about me <u>working there as a future employee</u>. She said that she would be thrilled if I took on the job. I was happy to hear that because I wanted to work there, but sad at the same time because I knew <u>I couldn't. I finally told her why I couldn't work there, and she couldn't believe that I couldn't do anything about getting a social security card, or a work permit to work legally here in the country.</u>

She began to ask me a lot of personal questions about my future and she became like a friend. I could see it in her eyes that she felt sorry for me. <u>I went to school and told my teacher what happened and she was also surprised because she did not know that I was undocumented.</u> All this happened about a week before I graduated, and she couldn't do much for me. <u>I felt so angry with God that last week of high school. I wanted to do so many things, but just because I am missing a series of numbers (social security number), I couldn't even have a good job.</u>

College

I graduated from high school and had some money saved up for college. It wasn't much different from high school, just more work in my first year at a Community College. <u>I was still searching for a way to get a social security card.</u> Someone had told me that <u>the easiest way to get one is to marry an American citizen</u>. At the time I did not feel I was ready to marry anyone. One day an old friend of mine from junior high called me and I was surprised because it had been such a long time since we last spoke. We started going out a lot and then became a couple. <u>He knew my situation and he wanted to do something to help me, so he asked me to marry him.</u>

I was so confused about everything but I wanted to get my green card so I accepted. I was already eighteen years old and I told my mom about my plans. She was concerned but thankfully, she stood by me and I got married. At the beginning of the marriage it was easy, but as time passed by it got harder and harder. My husband and I argued a lot about little things. Our communication was horrible, and sometimes we would not talk for days. He expected me to feed him, but I did not know how to cook. I had to drop out of school because I no longer had money or a job. We were always arguing about everything. I felt like I was in prison; I would just stay home and not do anything.

One day I talked to my friend Lupita, the one that got me my first job. She was working at a nightclub and she needed a girl like me to be a waitress. I was only eighteen and I knew it was illegal for me to be handling alcohol, but I needed the money, so I took the job. I started working there 16 hours a day, from 11 A.M. to 3 A.M. I even began to lose weight and I felt like a zombie. I was getting paid minimum wage plus tips. The money was all right, but it was the customers that I had a problem with. It was hard dealing with drunken people all the time. They would scream and curse at us waitresses and create fights.

They wanted to get more than just a simple, "Hi, how are you doing? Can I help you?" I saw many of my co-workers get spit on and harassed by the drunken customers. I was so young and saw very wrong things that people will do to each other. But I couldn't say anything, because again, I did not have the right to talk. I was undocumented and I had to always remain self-conscious about that.

Now I am twenty years old and working at a liquor store. My husband already petitioned for me to obtain legal status and our case is in progress. However, I am afraid because my lawyer told me that I have to leave this country in order to get my green card. But I'm scared to leave because I don't know anything about the outside (Mexico). I have heard that many of the people who go to Mexico to get their green card have been tricked and left over there with no way back.

I just wish there was an easier way of doing this, and I wish there was someone out there to help me. In conclusion, not all of us have the same luck. I always think things happen for a reason. Maybe God wants me to appreciate things better or maybe he is just giving me a hard time. Nothing comes easy in this life, and if you really want something, you have to go get it and do your best at it. I don't regret any of this because it's no one's fault.

Face To Face Interview

The second meeting served to verify, clarify, or add any additional information on the participants before any case study was written and data coded for salient descriptors and categorization into constructs or themes. Once all data was collected (semi-structured interviews, autobiographies, and face-to-face dialogue), the information was used to triangulate the data to establish meaning of participants lived experiences (Yin, 1984).

Brenda: Face-To-Face Interview

What comes to your mind as you reflect on this study? Taking part in this study on unauthorized college-age students has helped me realize many things that perhaps I did not before. I now see myself as <u>part of a struggle</u> and one that is <u>just.</u> I am very <u>limited</u> in where I can go and what I can do, like if I was <u>in jail,</u> but I have also learned to <u>adapt and even grow despite all these walls</u> around me. <u>I am going to college,</u> and that is more than many people who are born here.

It is amazing to me how <u>we have to constantly change to different situations,</u> never forgetting <u>who or what we are.</u> I cannot walk down the street without constantly been aware that <u>there are dangers all around me.</u> At any time I can be <u>detained, questioned, and deported.</u> If that would happen, I would be <u>separated from my family from all I have in my life</u>. So I try my best to <u>fit in and to not stand out.</u> I am <u>careful with what clothes I wear, where I go, and who I talk to</u>. I try to speak good English and not become alarmed when I see a border patrol agent or a policeman at the trolley stop. <u>Nervousness is one sure way to be caught.</u>

I know very well <u>the boundaries of my life.</u> I have a route that I follow every day. I do not leave that path. It would <u>be dangerous.</u> I know who and what I can <u>trust. I am a shadow in everyone's lives. No one notices me</u> because I do not protest <u>if I am treated unfairly.</u> I cannot call the police if I am in danger. I cannot even call the ambulance if I feel ill. We <u>walk around not existing, with no rights, no protection, no guarantees,</u> because I <u>don't belong</u> here; even though I have lived here most of my life, I do not belong. <u>We are all humans, but certainly not equal</u> if we are <u>not legal.</u> Life is hard.

I am <u>taking steps to try and get my documents.</u> I am now <u>married to a citizen</u> and we have filed the papers to start the process. I look forward <u>to not having to hide.</u> I look forward to working and buying things I want for my sisters, my mom, and me. When that moment comes, I want to become <u>active in the creation of change.</u> There are good and bad people everywhere.

I want to show people that <u>being illegal does not mean to be a criminal</u> or a bad person.

   More than ever, <u>I value my family,</u> even my life, because, despite it all, I am still luckier than others. It's difficult not <u>having access to things, not being able to go places, not being what you dream of being. I have no driver's license, no identity as an American,</u> but it's OK to dream right? Things could change, and, maybe one day, instead of <u>being seen as an illegal, I will simply be a college student and American.</u>

Index